SHORT-TERM TRADING

WITH

PRICE PATTERNS

A systematic methodology for
the development, testing, and use of
short-term trading systems

MICHAEL HARRIS

25th Anniversary
1975-2000

ISBN: 0-934380-60-0
Published January 2000

Editing, layout and cover design by
Kevin D. Stokes

25th Anniversary
1975-2000

TRADERS PRESS, INC.®
PO Box 6206
Greenville, SC 29606

Books and Gifts
for Investors and Traders

800-927-8222 / 864-298-0222   Fax 864-298-0221
Tradersprs@aol.com
http://www.traderspress.com

Publisher's note: the *System Writer Plus* software used to generate many of the tables appearing in this book is no longer available for purchase from Omega Research, Inc. It has since been replaced by *Omega Research TradeStation 2000i*, a comparable software package with enhanced performance capabilities. For additional information, please call 1-800-556-2022.

Visit our Website at http://www.traderspress.com

• View our latest releases
• Browse our updated catalog
• Access our gift shop for investors
• Read Ed Dobson's book reviews

Contact us for our 100-page catalog

25th Anniversary
1975-2000

TRADERS PRESS, INC.®
PO Box 6206
Greenville, SC 29606

Tradersprs@aol.com

800-927-8222

Fax 864-298-0222

To my parents, George and Dorothy.

- M.H.

TRADERS PRESS, INC. ®

Publishers of:

A Complete Guide to Trading Profits (Paris)
A Professional Look at S&P Day Trading (Trivette)
Ask Mr. EasyLanguage (Tennis)
Beginner's Guide to Computer Assisted Trading (Alexander)
Channels and Cycles: A Tribute to J.M. Hurst (Millard)
Chart Reading for Professional Traders (Jenkins)
Commodity Spreads: Analysis, Selection and Trading Techniques (Smith)
Comparison of Twelve Technical Trading Systems (Lukac, Brorsen, & Irwin)
Cyclic Analysis (J.M. Hurst)
Day Trading with Short Term Price Patterns (Crabel)
Exceptional Trading: The Mind Game (Roosevelt)
Fibonacci Ratios with Pattern Recognition (Pesavento)
Geometry of Markets (Gilmore)
Geometry of Stock Market Profits (Jenkins)
Harmonic Vibrations (Pesavento)
How to Trade in Stocks (Livermore)
Hurst Cycles Course (J.M. Hurst)
Jesse Livermore: Speculator King (Sarnoff)
Magic of Moving Averages (Lowry)
Pit Trading: Do You Have the Right Stuff? (Hoffman & Baccetti)
Planetary Harmonics of Speculative Markets (Pesavento)
Point & Figure Charting (Aby)
Point & Figure Charting: Commodity and Stock Trading Techniques (Zieg)
Profitable Grain Trading (Ainsworth)
Profitable Pattern for Stock Trading (Pesavento)
Stock Market Trading Systems (Appel & Hitschler)
Stock Patterns for Day Trading (Rudd)
Stock Patterns for Day Trading 2 (Rudd)
Study Helps in Point & Figure Techniques (Wheelan)
Technically Speaking (Wilkinson)
Technical Trading Systems for Commodities and Stocks (Patel)
The Amazing Life of Jesse Livermore (Smitten)
The Professional Commodity Trader (Kroll)
The Taylor Trading Technique (Taylor)
The Traders (Kleinfeld)
*The Trading Rule That Can Make You Rich** (Dobson)
Traders Guide to Technical Analysis (Hardy)
Trading Secrets of the Inner Circle (Goodwin)
Trading S&P Futures and Options (Lloyd)
Understanding Bollinger Bands (Dobson)
Understanding Fibonacci Numbers (Dobson)
Viewpoints of a Commodity Trader (Longstreet)
Wall Street Ventures & Adventures Through Forty Years (Wyckoff)
Winning Market Systems (Appel)

Contents

SECTION ONE
Background

Contents

SECTION TWO
Trading with Short-term Price Patterns

Contents

Preface

Making money by trading futures is probably the most difficult task one can undertake. It requires devotion, discipline and continuous research. In order to achieve the objective of becoming a profitable trader, one has to make several sacrifices in his or her personal life and must go through the painful process of testing several ideas in actual trading. This may be a very costly endeavor, but is also one that can bring financial independence.

There are different ways to achieve success, whether through a mechanical trading system or a fundamental approach to the markets. What seems to count most at the end of the day is not so much the particular method used, but the methodology itself. Most traders have spent long hours in modeling and testing trading systems, but few have spent the time and effort to develop a specific methodology and trading style. This may sound a little abstract, but years of experience have shown that a trading methodology is as important as the trading system itself. Of course, implementation and execution of a trading methodology require knowledge and experience that few possess, as well as a discipline that even fewer exercise. Those very few who combine both are the long-term winners.

Writing a book requires a lot of effort, but it is a very important step in the author's life. It is a turning point, like reaching the end of a highway and looking for a new direction to take. It is also a motivation to turn to new ways and investigate new frontiers. That is the beauty of sharing past knowledge and experience with others.

M. H.

Acknowledgments

The author wishes to thank the following individuals:

Ed Dobson and his staff at Traders Press, Inc., for taking a chance on a first-time writer.

Averill Strasser - For providing motivation for the completion of this manuscript through his independent evaluation of the author's research work.

Neil Weintraub - For his invaluable input with information on publishing a book, desperately needed by a new author.

Artemis Pulaka - For her invaluable input and assistance in preparing the manuscript.

List of Figures

List of Tables

Introduction

This book was written with two objectives in mind: to provide futures traders with specific trading systems, and to provide a methodology to employ these trading systems in systematic trading. Both of these elements working in synergy are required to win in futures trading. An effective trading system puts in place the prospect of profitable trading. In turn, a skilled trader uses a trading methodology to take advantage of this prospect in a way that is appropriate and is consistent with the requirements of the trading system in use. This harmonious cooperation of the trader/system combination will eventually lead to consistent long-term profits.

The reader will notice an absence of unnecessary illustrations of historical price charts. Only those absolutely necessary to explain the concepts presented have been included. Nowadays every trader has some means of looking at historical charts, including several daily publications and the Internet. There is no need to buy a book to do that! Furthermore, I avoid stating qualitative trading rules such as "the trend is your friend…" etc. Most of us have heard or shared many rules that must be followed in order to be a successful trader; these sayings are often of general context and are even contradictory at times. What are rarely heard or shown are specific methodologies and systems that make money in a consistent and systematic way.

The global financial system, an important part of which is the futures markets, is a very complex, dynamic process. Advances in technology have facilitated the rapid flow of funds between investment vehicles that can be located on opposite sides of the globe. It seems difficult for even the most well-educated, well-trained human minds to predict the movement of capital in a way that will lead to systematic gains. Sudden reversals in the direction of market prices can make previous hard-earned gains disappear in a matter of hours, or even turn into devastating losses. Recouping the losses can be a difficult task.

The systems and methods shown in this book attempt to deal with the nature of the futures markets by adopting a short-term trading approach based on historical price patterns. These patterns can be easily programmed in the computer and monitored on a daily basis. Positions may be placed either on the close of the day that the pattern formation is completed or at the open of the next trading day. A profit target and a stop loss are placed immediately, as soon as the position is established. The average duration of a trade can vary from one to a few days, depending on the profit and loss objectives of the particular patterns employed in the trading system model.

This book is divided into three sections. Section One, entitled "Background," provides a review of basic concepts. In chapter 1 I describe the differences between the various time frames used in trading futures. In chapter 2 I review the trading methods and techniques employed by traders, and in chapter 3 I discuss the data requirements of trading. Those first three chapters also provide a rationale and justification for the selection of short-term trading as the trading style most suitable for systematic trading, which is further elaborated in chapter 4. In chapter 5 I present a comprehensive framework for modeling and simulating trading systems, a step-by-step procedure to be followed by the trading system developer. This framework increases the probability that the trading system models developed will behave the same way in real life as during the simulation procedure.

Finally, in chapter 6, I give a specific example of how to model, simulate and improve the performance of a trading system. These last two chapters of Section One provide the necessary background to develop consistently winning trading systems using the concepts presented in the remainder of the book.

Section Two, entitled "Trading With Short-term Price Patterns," deals with the development of short-term trading system models based on historical price patterns. In chapter 7 I outline a procedure for price pattern searching based on a trial-and-error method. Then I present a methodology for developing short-term trading systems that are collections of short-term price patterns, and for using those trading systems to generate daily trading signals in a systematic way. In chapter 8 I classify short-term price patterns into different types, depending on their properties. Chapter 9 introduces the idea of automating the search for historical price patterns; in chapter 10 I present a general approach to short-term trading using an automated pattern search. Chapter 11 deals with money management techniques and focuses on the estimation of trading capital and risk. In Chapter 12 I discuss advanced ways of using short-term patterns by taking into consideration some special situations that often arise. Finally, in chapter 13 I introduce the p-Indicator, a short-term trading indicator based on historical price patterns—the first one of its kind.

Section Three is a library of specific price patterns, for several commodity futures, which have been found using the automatic pattern search method I have developed. I describe the chart formation, performance characteristics, and programming logic of each pattern listed, so it can be readily used in a trading system model. This is the first time ever that such a great number of short-term price patterns have been revealed in a single publication.

The methods and techniques presented in this book are the result of extensive research and development. The computer programs used to discover the short-term price patterns listed in Section Three have taken many years to develop, and substantial resources have been devoted to that effect. I certainly hope that the reader will be motivated by this work and will proceed to develop his or her own methods and techniques of trading, using the concepts presented here as a foundation. After all, trading is a personal endeavor, one that requires a combination of hard work and continuing effort. Let us keep this last comment in mind while turning the page to Section One.

SECTION ONE

BACKGROUND

Basic Concepts

This section is a review of a few basic concepts useful to anyone who is involved or is planning to get involved in developing a mechanical trading system. Although very basic and seemingly trivial, these concepts play a crucial role in the development of a successful trading system and its correct application to real-life trading. A lack of their understanding often results in a faulty system and in trading losses. For example, a trading system developer must understand the concepts of *trading time frames, trading techniques* used and *information requirements* that accompany them. A trend-following system, for instance, is designed to follow long-term price movements, and should not be used for intraday trading purposes. Furthermore, an intraday trader must understand the need for a real-time price quote system and must pay the associated cost. As much as one may think that these are obvious conclusions, during my trading years I have come across several traders who attempted to use a trend following system for intraday trading purposes, and others who managed to trade very heavily on an intraday basis by looking at the delayed futures price updates of a television station business program. Needless to say what happened to their trading capital...

The following is a list of the basic concepts that must be understood by a trading system developer:

Trading Time Frames
Trading Methods
Data Requirements
Systems Modeling
Simulation

Chapter One

Trading Time Frames

The Trading Time Frame refers to the average duration that a trading system is designed to stay in a position, long or short. In principle, we can distinguish three different time frames: intraday, short term and longer term. What is important, from the trading system designer's point of view, is that the modeling and analysis process may differ, depending on the time frame selected with which to operate. Likewise, the daily trading system requirements, in terms of data needed for operation and discipline on the part of the trader, will also vary. Here I attempt to explain these differences and to cast some light on this seemingly trivial but often confusing subject.

Intraday Trading

In intraday trading, individual trades can last from a few seconds to several hours. Usually an intraday trader establishes a "flat" position by market close and does not carry open positions overnight.

In order to develop an intraday trading system one must use historical intraday data. Although some developers make the point that intraday data looks like daily data, nothing can replace the validity of the performance results obtained by using actual historical intraday data.

The past performance of an intraday trading system must be back-tested using several years worth of data. Although historical intraday data is widely available by several vendors, its integrity is often questionable. A more reliable source to obtain intraday data is directly from the exchanges, or from authorized re-sellers that use the exchange "Time and Sales" records to extract the data.

Even if a profitable intraday trading system is successfully designed, its actual operation may vary significantly from simulated use. There are two basic reasons for this: slippage and market liquidity. Slippage is the variation between the price that a mechanical trading system indicates that an order is filled and the actual fill price. In simulated trading system performance the slippage cannot be estimated or even closely approximated because the actual trading conditions are simply not known. Although simulation packages allow for the inclusion of slippage as a parameter in the design process, "fast" markets can result in huge deviations from expected values. This may easily wipe out a streak of winning trades and leave the trading account in the red. In order to account for such conditions, the designer must perform statistical analysis based on random slippage variable inputs—an academic researcher's task, beyond the handle of the average developer.

Market liquidity, when low, can significantly alter the performance of an intraday trading system. In many instances, during intraday position initiation, the opposite side of the trade is the floor trader. Undoubtedly, when competing with the floor trader the winning chances are very small. One reason for this is that the floor broker is in a better position to know the "order flow" in the exchange and, under certain conditions, can "move" the market in a specific direction, enough to "stop-out" an intraday trader. This is especially true if the floor broker is a market maker and operates in a slow and illiquid market. This phenomenon should not be viewed as market inefficiency; it is just the way the markets work. Nonetheless, the net effect on an intraday trading system's performance can be profound.

The methods and techniques used to activate buy and sell signals in intraday systems, as well as to offset open positions, vary from simple and intuitive to very mathematical and algorithmic. The use of technical indicators in intraday trading system modeling is widespread, but their effectiveness is questionable. One reason is that most of the indicators are, by design, intended to "smooth" or "average" the data. That results in the loss of volatility and a lagging effect in tracking actual price moves. Chart patterns and analysis can be more effective for such applications. Intuitive methods may include conditions such as the time of the day, the day of the week, the tick volume, price change momentum, etc.

Commission size is very important in intraday trading. Total commissions paid accumulate fast and by the end of the trading year can amount to a significant percentage of the initial trading capital. This can be studied during trading system simulation by varying the commission variable. In my experience, it is very difficult to be a profitable intraday trader if round turn commission is higher than $12 per contract traded.

Someone could ask, "If that is so difficult, why do people trade intraday?" There are a few answers to this question, depending on someone's experience of the markets and of other traders. Based on my own experience, I have never met an intraday trader who made money consistently for a long period of time. The explanation I attempt to give for this is that intraday trading is a full-time occupation that requires the discipline of staying long hours in front of the real-time data screen and trying to follow a trading plan without being fooled by the illusive moves of the market. At some point even the strongest deviate from their trading plan. Such deviation often results in irrational moves on the part of the trader, motivated simply by greed and hope that the market will move in a certain direction...

Short-term Trading

In short-term trading, the trade duration may be one to several days. In essence, a short-term trader tries to "time" the direction of the short-term price moves of a specific market. In principle this problem deals with market timing, but being successful requires more than that. The reason is that in the short term, markets move mostly in a random fashion. The objective of a short-term trading system must be to determine the times when there is a high probability that the market will move in a specific direction, the long-term trend or direction of prices being unimportant. This can only be done effectively in a systematic fashion; i.e., there is a need for a consistently winning trading system that exhibits appropriate performance characteristics.

The use of trading formulas and indicators in short-term trading is very questionable. Formulas such as moving averages and indicators such as Relative Strength Index and Directional Moving Index cannot be used effectively in short-term trading. The time lag that these mathematical algorithms exhibit in following short-term moves is just too long to allow their effective use. By the time a position is established the market often reverses direction and that results in a trading loss. That is the reason why an effective method of trading short term is via *historical price patterns*. Those patterns are like the well-known chart patterns but are more exact in form and often simpler in structure. Traditional chart patterns like heads & shoulders, double bottoms and triangles are often subjective formations that may be more useful in establishing market turning points than short-term price direction. Unlike those traditional chart patterns, historical price patterns are more difficult to spot but are, by nature, suitable for use in short-term trading.

Commission paid is rarely an issue in short-term trading. Slippage does not affect real performance if the profit target and stop loss are kept at reasonably high levels. Furthermore, a short-term trading system can be designed (and this is often the case) to establish positions at the close of the trading day or at the open of the next day, making the presence of a real-time data feed unnecessary. And when a position is established, long or short, a profit target and a stop loss can be entered as an open position order. That leaves free time for the trader, as opposed to intraday trading, which requires the trader to watch the data screen constantly.

In order to be successful in short-term trading, a system must be developed that is capable of predicting short-term price direction. Designing such a system is not a trivial task. If historical price patterns are used, discovering those patterns is a time-consuming process that requires extensive use of the computer. Although this is a difficult task, if done properly the result can be a consistently winning trading system that is much easier to trade than an intraday or long-term "trend-following system."

Longer-term Trading

Longer-term trading, or what I often refer to as "trend" trading, is about capturing or following a trend in prices, in either the long or short direction. It is also called "trend following." Trade duration can be weeks or even several months. The trader may choose to slowly accumulate contracts, making long-term trading by far the method with the highest profit potential—at least theoretically. In real life there are a few basic problems that often turn this stellar prospect into a disappointing endeavor. The first is that a price trend can only be identified after it has been formed! This is often called "hindsight." In addition, the end of a trend is never known soon enough, but only when there is a considerable retracement in prices or a trend reversal! The paradox is that in hindsight, indicators are almost perfect instruments for following trends. They are not effective, however, in establishing the trend top or bottom; thus, a system developer must rely on methods such as trailing stops. The problem with trailing stops is that the volatility during and at the end of the trend is not known in advance. Low values of the trailing stop take the system out of the trend too soon and high values subject it to a huge loss at the end of the trend, when prices reverse direction.

Trend-trading systems can be designed with the use of either daily or weekly data. A real-time data feed to monitor the markets on an intraday basis is not required and the trader can have another occupation at the same time. However, even if the basic design problems of trend trading systems are solved, real life application requires extreme discipline to be exercised by the trader. Very few traders have the patience to maintain profitable positions for long periods of time, as one is often tempted to pocket short-term gains as soon as they occur. As a matter of fact, I have known very few individuals who have successfully followed a trend, even partially, and profited from that! It is by far the most difficult style of trading to implement and execute in real life.

Summary

Selection of the trading time frame is a very important first step in the development of a successful mechanical trading system. The selection criteria must be based on the objectives of the trader, after considering carefully the requirements imposed in terms of daily monitoring and execution. Intraday and short-term trading are recommended only if one plans to become a full-time trader. Otherwise a trend-trading system must be considered.

Chapter Two

Trading Methods

There are two basic methods that traders employ in their decision process: fundamental and technical. Although the two can be combined, it is often the case that traders who use fundamental methods rarely use technical methods and traders who are technically oriented know little about how to use fundamental methods correctly. In my opinion, this is possibly due to the very different educational background of the two trader types, the fundamental user being most often an economist and the technical anything but an economist. Irrespective of a trader's background and method used, success comes only if there is a deep understanding of the factors and parameters involved and their correct application in trading the markets.

Fundamental Methods

Fundamental methods are based on the consideration, analysis and subsequent quantification of the economic, social and political factors that affect demand and supply in the markets. Fundamental methods can have an application in long-term trading but are ineffective in intraday and short-term trading. There

13

are many reasons for this, including the limited availability of economic data in a timely fashion and the inability to predict monetary policy actions on time. Then there are cases of unexpected events, such as wars or political decisions, which have a decisive impact on market price direction.

Often fundamentals are used to make long-term investment or economic policy decisions in Fixed Income, Currency and Equity Markets. Occasionally fundamentals are used to establish long-term positions in Commodity or Derivative products. The failure in late 1998 of Hedge Funds, which based trading on fundamental methods, suggests that more work needs to be done in this area.

Technical Methods

Technical methods are based on the use of mathematical formulas known as studies or indicators, the analysis of chart patterns, or combinations of both. The objective is to predict future price direction only, although some chart patterns attempt to also predict the magnitude of the price change. An example is the so-called "flag" chart formation.

Indicators such as the Directional Moving Index have smoothing properties, essentially average prices, and thus are not suitable for short-term trading due to the time lag they exhibit in tracking actual price moves. This is especially noticeable in "choppy" markets, where indicators are unable to perform. However, indicators can be excellent tools for trend following, if properly applied.

Charting methods can apply to intraday and short-term trading but their effectiveness is very limited. Most traditional chart patterns, like double tops or bottoms and flags, are very difficult to spot and confirmation of their formation comes very late in the price move, leaving very little room for profits. Historical price patterns can be very effective in both intraday and short-term trading. There is, however, a very important assumption made that "history repeats itself." Therefore, in order to use these types of patterns correctly, one must first discover them and then study their performance characteristics very carefully. This is the subject of extensive work to be done by the trading system developer, the result of which can be very rewarding.

Technical methods can be very valuable tools if used with extreme caution. Unexpected events outside the scope of technical analysis can trigger price movements that result in severe losses. It is therefore necessary to study the historical performance of any technical method considered before applying it under real trading conditions. This, of course, assumes that the technical method can be fully described in a way that can be implemented in the computer. Chapter 5 makes further reference to this subject.

A Combination of Methods

Several unsuccessful attempts are made, from time to time, to combine fundamental and technical methods. My opinion is that such a combination is very difficult due to the fact that the two methods deal with very different parameters and have very different objectives. Furthermore, although some economic data series can be integrated with historical price data and subsequently applied to trading system models, their usefulness is highly questionable. One reason for this is that technical methods and analysis already assume that prices at any given moment reflect the prevailing economic conditions. Thus the use of economic data is redundant unless one expects that a surprise in the magnitude of an economic data release is forthcoming. If this is the case then the unexpected event probably will be hard to quantify and model. Furthermore, the market swings are so violent and fast when such an event occurs that trading anything becomes very difficult.

In my experience, the combination of technical and fundamental methods can have merit in trend trading but is to be avoided in intraday and short-term trading. Furthermore, the inclusion of fundamental factors in a trading model often causes the trader to direct attention to the daily development of such events. This type of focus may result in forming a personal opinion about market direction, which can be used to alter the decision process of the trading system. Although this topic could be the subject of an interesting debate, it is outside the scope of this book, which concentrates exclusively on systematic trading via the use of a mechanical trading system model based on technical methods.

Summary

Fundamental or technical methods may be used for market forecasting. Development of mechanical trading systems requires the use of technical methods that can be fully described in a way that can be implemented in the computer. Depending on the trading time frame employed, the proper technical trading method must be applied in order to obtain desirable performance.

Chapter Three

Data Requirements

Data requirements may vary significantly during both the development phase and the actual trading, depending on the type of the trading system developed and used.

Intraday trading systems require the use of historical intraday data in their performance analysis, and a real-time data feed during actual trading operation. If the trader uses the real-time feed to collect intraday data then maintenance should be performed regularly in order to find and remove spikes that are due to faulty transmissions. It is advisable to update the intraday data files on a regular basis using a reliable vendor that checks for data integrity. If corrupted data files are used in historical simulation, it is possible that the performance results obtained will be misleading.

Short-term trading systems require daily historical data during simulation and performance analysis. Daily trading requires either real-time or end-of-day data, depending on the specific structure of the system used. If the trading system initiates positions either at the close of today or at the open of the next day and uses a fixed profit target and stop loss, then end-of-day data is sufficient. If a short-term trading system initiates positions during the trading day, then a real-time feed may be necessary.

Updating and maintaining daily data files can be done in several ways, depending on the number of futures contracts traded. There are many vendors of end-of-day data that provide a reliable update shortly after market closing. Traders who monitor prices for just a few contracts often make manual updating.

Trend trading systems can be simulated using either daily or weekly data, depending on the requirements. An end-of-day data service is more than sufficient for daily operation. Some trend traders even use the daily newspaper and manually update their data files.

Irrespective of the methods used to update and maintain data files, careful attention should be given to any adjustments that must be regularly made to the data. The proper data Time Series must be used during both the development and the daily execution of a trading system. If continuously adjusted data is used, proper adjustments must be made to past prices during the rollover of future contracts, in order to insure correct operation of those systems. Most trading software packages that facilitate trading system implementation and monitoring allow those adjustments to be made to the data in a relatively easy way. If the proper adjustments are not made, the trader risks compromising the operation of the trading system.

Chapter Four

The Case for Short-term Trading

Table 4-1 shows a summary of the basic concepts discussed in chapters 1 through 3. One conclusion that may be made from the comparisons on the table is that short-term trading is the only trading time frame that is better suitable to a systematic trading system approach while minimizing other requirements such as daily work needed to be performed and discipline to be exercised. I reach this conclusion by noting that short-term trading requires the presence of a trading system model whereas the other trading time frames can use fundamental and intuitive techniques. Although it is not a simple task to develop a winning trading system model, if successful in doing that, the developer puts in place the basic and necessary ingredient for systematic trading. That, of course, does not exclude the possibility that trading systems can be developed and used successfully based on other trading time frames. Furthermore, a trader is free to use a combination of systems that operate in different time frames.

My own opinion and experience is that regardless of the techniques employed, consistent and long-term profitability can only be achieved via the systematic use of a trading system model.

TIME FRAME	DATA NEEDS	TECHNIQUES	PROS	CONS
INTRADAY SECONDS TO HOURS	REAL-TIME	PATTERNS INDICATORS INTUITIVE	NO OVERNIGHT POSITIONS	COMPETITION WITH THE FLOOR TRADER; HIGH COMMISSION AND SLIPPAGE; FULL-TIME OCCUPATION
SHORT-TERM ONE TO A FEW DAYS	REAL-TIME OR END-OF-DAY	PATTERNS	FEW TRADES; WELL-DEFINED TARGETS AND STOPS	NEED A TRADING MODEL
TREND WEEKS TO MONTHS	END-OF-DAY OR WEEKLY	INDICATORS FUNDAMENTAL	HIGH PROFITS WHEN ADDING TO POSITION; LOW COMMISSION	NEED DISCIPLINE; EXITS NOT KNOWN

Table 4-1: Comparisons of Trading Time Frames

Section two of this book concentrates specifically on the development of short-term trading systems which are based on historical price patterns, and on the use of methodologies that facilitate systematic trading under actual market conditions.

Chapter Five

Modeling and Simulation of Trading Systems

The availability of high-speed personal computers at low cost has made possible the modeling and simulation of trading systems by anyone with basic programming skills. Two decades ago, this could only be done by those who had access to expensive mainframe machines, as well as an understanding of special computer programming skills. Today, individuals can buy software packages that provide a general platform for the implementation and simulation of trading systems, using high-level programming languages specifically designed for that purpose.

My own view is that all this technological progress has increased the complexity of trading and the amount of effort needed in order to become a successful system trader. Furthermore, despite all the advances, modeling and simulation of trading systems remains a highly technical and specialized field that requires actual trading experience combined with knowledge of mathematics, statistics and computer programming. Lack of an in-depth understanding of the underlying concepts and techniques results in faulty trading system models.

Trading System Modeling

A *model* is a description of some system designed to predict what happens if certain actions are taken. The process of determining the model is called *modeling*. The result of modeling is often put in a mathematical form, so that it looks like a formula, a set of equations or logical propositions, or a mixture thereof. The are at least two types of models: abstract and empirical. *Abstract* models are based on *a priori* knowledge of the actual operation of the system to be modeled. *Empirical* models are based on experiments and observations.

The following is an example of a trading model:

If the close of today is higher than the value of the moving average of the last two days' highs then buy one contract today on the close with profit target at the fill price plus one point and protective stop at the fill price minus one point.

As shown in figure 5-1, the market can be thought of as a system that is comprised of all entities that participate in it, called the traders. The input to the system consists of news, information about this market and other markets, and future expectations about price levels, amongst other things. The output of the system is the price of a particular asset and has three possible levels: up, down or steady. That is true whether one considers the next trade, the next second, five minutes, the day of the week or the month of the year.

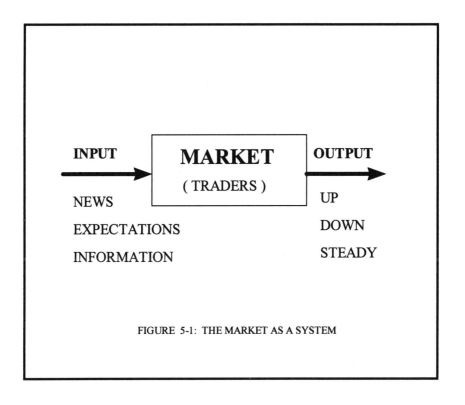

FIGURE 5-1: THE MARKET AS A SYSTEM

Although the output states of the system in figure 5-1 are few in number and simple in nature, what generates them is a highly non-linear and stochastic process that is essentially the result-ant of all the individual processes that characterize the deci-sions of each participating trader in the system. By simply know-ing the past history of the output states of this system, it is im-possible to come up with a mathematical model that will ap-proximate its future behavior to any satisfactory degree. It is just so complex that it is beyond the scope of mathematical science as we know it today. But even if a model could be constructed, the inputs that drive it cannot be known in advance, as to generate the output states for the next time interval. And to make things even more complicated, the market often exhibits an anticipatory behavior, meaning that the output states at a specific time may depend on expectations about the future values of the inputs. This further complicates the process and makes the task of finding a model for the market a very difficult (perhaps even impossible) task.

In practice, one can construct an approximate model for the market, in the sense that the model output will coincide with the actual market output on certain instances, called the "Entry Points" or "Trading Signals." During those instances, non-linear and random effects will, presumably, be minimized and will have a reduced effect on market behavior. This can allow simpler deterministic system models to be a satisfactory approximation of the real non-linear and stochastic system. As input to our model, we can use the past price history of the market, a time series of prices of appropriate length that depends on the particular model used, as shown in Figure 5-2.

In principle, the intention and desire of the system developer is that the sum of all losses, or losing trades, will be smaller than the sum of all gains, or profitable trades, that are generated by the system over a long period of time.

Modeling a trading system is more of an art than a science. Determining what is important to include or exclude from the model requires an in-depth knowledge of the inner workings of the underlying process. Although many trading system developers treat markets as time series where the object is to make a forecast or prediction, the result is often a trading system that cannot be used in real-life trading. An example of this is intraday trading systems that are developed by analyzing a time series of historical prices based on a few minute price intervals or bars. Such time series are unrealistic to use since order placing and execution cannot take place instantaneously, as these systems assume when modeled and simulated. This is not a question of slippage, but rather a fault in the model design to account for actual trading conditions.

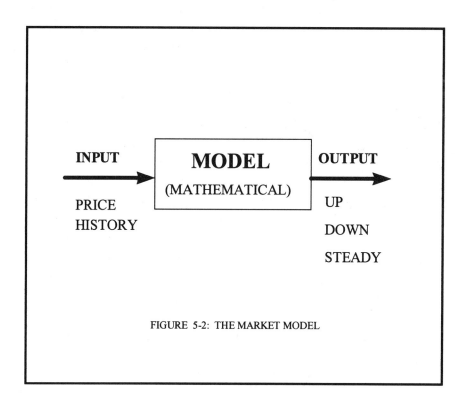

FIGURE 5-2: THE MARKET MODEL

Trading System Model Simulation

Simulation is the process of driving a model with input and observing its output. Often, when a model of a trading system is available, the object of the simulation is to use as the input a time series of historical prices and to obtain a set of trade entry and exit points, as shown Figure 5-3. The entry and exit points, labeled E_i and X_i respectively, can then be used in conjunction with the known input to calculate a set of performance parameters useful in evaluating the model performance. The process of simulating the historical performance of a trading system model with input made of actual historical data is also called "back testing" or "historical testing."

The input to the trading system model can be made of tick, intraday of any period length, weekly or even monthly data. Combinations of these can also be used. As soon as the performance of the trading system model is obtained under actual historical conditions, the data can be filtered out or altered using random inputs, in order to study the effect on the model performance. Time series of prices with appropriate characteristics can also be made up, using a time series generator. It is my opinion, however, that testing a trading system model under such hypothetical conditions is not as useful as testing it under actual historical conditions, unless the developer aims at studying the model robustness with random inputs. It is very difficult to make any conclusions about performance based on events that have never occurred, simply because it is not known how the actual market would have behaved, or whether those hypothetical inputs actually would have been generated by the market.

The criteria for evaluating performance results obtained by the simulation are very subjective and depend on the trading objectives of the developer. One can construct many performance parameters that can be calculated using the simulation results. Those are often called "statistics." In Table 5-1, six most commonly used parameters are listed.

Aside from the statistics listed in Table 5-1, there are other, more basic and intuitive ones that can be studied using the simulation results and a basic statistics software program. One example is the distribution of returns and of actual entry points. These distributions can give the developer a picture of the behavior of the model output and a feeling for its usefulness in actual trading conditions.

PARAMETER	DESCRIPTION
N	Total number of trades generated
%P	Percent profitable trades
R_{WL}	Ratio of average winning to loss
C_L	Maximum consecutive losers
T_D	Average time in a trade
D_R	Maximum draw down

Table 5-1: Commonly Used Performance Statistics

In simple language, as to demystify statistics, if a significant portion of the gains of a trading system model (simulated, for instance, over a period of ten years) occur within a specific, short period of time (let us say one month), then even if the performance is acceptable, the model may not be, depending again on trading objectives. This is especially important to fund managers who would like to demonstrate as smooth an equity line as possible. Another intuitive measure is to observe the distribution of entry points over time. This distribution must be as uniform as possible, meaning that the system operates under all market conditions, throughout the simulation period. This is especially desirable in the case of short-term trading models where the duration of a trade is on the order of a few days.

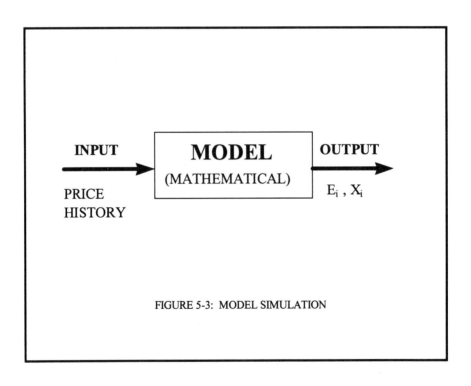

INPUT

PRICE
HISTORY

MODEL
(MATHEMATICAL)

OUTPUT

E_i , X_i

FIGURE 5-3: MODEL SIMULATION

As with modeling, simulation is more of an art than a science. Interpretation of the results obtained can only be made in the context of the model's intended operation. The results, in absolute terms, may mean very little. That is why the developer must always keep the modeling goals in perspective and must never be fooled by results that appear to be good but seem not to be justified by the model's intended operation. Good simulation results do not always imply a good system to trade.

Modeling and Simulation Procedure

Trading system developers with many years of modeling and simulation experience know that the process of finding a profitable mechanical trading system is not an easy one and has many pitfalls along the way. Here I attempt to clarify this subject and point out some problem areas.

Figure 5-4 shows a block diagram of the modeling and simulation steps which need to be followed in order to increase the chances of developing a truly winning trading system that performs the way it is intended to.

Modeling:

Trading models can be described as abstract mathematical forms, as empirical logical propositions, or as a combination of both. Initially the developer must try to isolate the basic premise that the model operation is based on and must implement a structure of minimal complexity. This facilitates a step-by-step modeling process with easier checking for any modeling errors. Furthermore, if the basic idea that the model is based on generates disappointing results, increasing the complexity of the model by adding to it will not necessarily make it perform better.

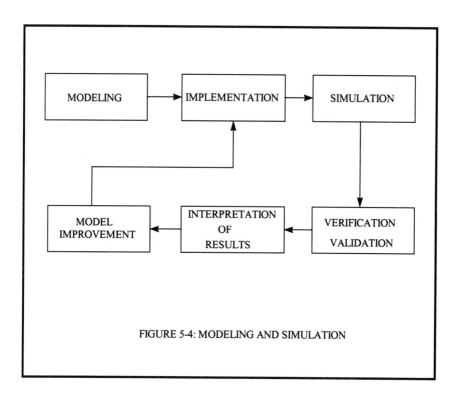

FIGURE 5-4: MODELING AND SIMULATION

The number of variables that can be adjusted, or optimized, must be kept to an absolute minimum. As a matter of fact, one should avoid the use of any variables in a trading model, if possible. Of course, that is impossible when employing indicators or mathematical formulas such as moving averages. In that case, a safe approach is to obtain performance results for wide ranges of those parameters that are acceptable to a reasonable extent. If the results have wide variations and even show negative performance for a small change in parameter values, then that is an indication of over-optimization or "fitting," and the model structure must be re-evaluated.

The short-term price patterns that are listed in section three do not have any variables to be optimized or varied. I refer to them as "pure," meaning that they are simple structures made up of daily price variations. Their modeling is very simple, and that minimizes the possibility of modeling and implementation errors.

Model Implementation:

Implementation means describing the model in a way that can be understood by the computer. In order to do that the developer must write computer code. This can be accomplished by either writing code based on any popular programming language or using available trading system development software packages. The latter provide a general platform for describing and simulating trading models in a high-level language. They have a built-in database of market prices, indicator formulas, or even ready-made trading system modules. Their presentation capabilities are often stunning, providing excellent graphics and performance analysis results. Although they may sound like a bargain, these packages have several inherent limitations that are often unknown to the novice user. Therefore, one must become very proficient with the use of these packages before anything significant can be developed. Put simply, the degree of proficiency is directly proportional to the time spent using those packages. Experience has shown that it takes about two to three years of learning curve to become an efficient trading system developer. That may vary depending on background and previous experience.

Model Simulation:

The object of simulation is to drive the model with historical data and generate a set of entry and exit points. This simplest form of simulation is also called "back testing." Using the entry and exit points generated, a set of model performance parameters can be calculated. In order for those parameters to have statistical significance, a sufficient span of historical input data must be used. In addition, the output of the model must generate enough entry and exit points. It is recommended that the whole available price history be used as input data. In terms of the model output, the number of entry and exit points that is sufficient depends on the trading system time frame. Trend-following trading models can be allowed to generate fewer trades as compared with short-term and intraday models. The sufficient number of output points is a debatable subject.

Many (mostly novice) trading system developers take a quick look at the simulation results and decide in a few seconds whether that is a good system to trade or not. However, unacceptable results can also be due to errors in the model programming implementation or errors in the modeling itself. In any case, there are more steps to be followed in the development of a successful trading system.

Model Verification:

After the simulation run, the developer must verify that the model operates the way it is supposed to. Due to programming limitations in the software program used or errors in the modeling and coding, the results can be quite different than they should. To verify the trading model results, the developer must take several batches of random data and make manual calculations. Likewise, entry and exit points must be selected at random and checked manually to determine if their presence is compatible with the model logic.

Verification is a time-consuming and tedious step in the development process. Its importance, however, should not be overlooked or underestimated. As a developer gets more familiar with trading system modeling and simulation, it may not be absolutely necessary to check the calculations manually. However, it is recommended to always select more than one entry and exit point and investigate their validity, in spite of the simplicity of a trading model's logic. Often, trivial errors can produce very misleading results.

Model Validation:

Validation problems arise when there is a disparity between the model software operation and the way the model operates in real trading. For example, problems caused by the so-called "Temporal Aggregation" phenomenon can significantly affect the actual model performance. This particular problem arises when different events occur during the same simulation period, let us say a daily bar. Widely used modeling and simulation packages make gross assumptions when encountering such problems. An example is when both a stop and a profit target are hit during the same simulation bar, whether that is a five-minute, a daily or a weekly period. Most software packages assume that the stop is filled first, which is a worst-case scenario. In order to study the effects of this phenomenon on the model performance, the developer must use intuitive measures and techniques. For instance, one can vary the magnitudes of the profit target and stop and note the corresponding performance. If the profitability of the model increases or decreases significantly then that indicates certain instability and the model logic must be carefully reconsidered. Another, more complicated way is to use second data input, with smaller time period bars, in conjunction with the model input. At least one vendor of a popular software package available in the market has realized this problem and allows for multiple time periods in a simulation. Nevertheless, the validation step is a very important one and there are not any generic procedures for approaching it. The developer must rely on past experience for that.

Interpretation of Results:

The simulation results must be studied carefully in order to decide whether the trading system model can be employed under actual trading conditions. The magnitude of the performance statistics generated must be analyzed in the context of the model objectives and the developer trading objectives. A trend-following system, for instance, must be allowed, by nature, to have a higher number of consecutive losers than a short-term trading system. There are no "rigid" guidelines for this number, and the effect is the plurality of trading systems that exist in the market, many claiming to possess good performance characteristics.

Besides the performance statistics that are commonly generated and studied, the developer may look at several others that can be of an intuitive nature, but are often very useful. As an example I can mention the distribution of quarterly returns. This data can be obtained easily with the use of a simple statistics software package or a spreadsheet. The information presented by a simple graph like that is often very useful. In any event, interpretation of the simulation results is a very subjective process that improves as the experience of the developer increases.

Model Improvement:

This is a step in the process where caution must be exercised. Many developers spot the worst trades generated by their trading model and try to employ schemes that will help to eliminate them. This is no longer model improvement but more a way of trying to fit model performance to someone's expectations. Losing trades are not necessarily bad, if followed by a streak of winning trades. By adding more variables and parameters to the model, one risks the elimination of good trades and a reduction in model performance. If a way to improve the model results in a severe reduction in the expected number of trades, then that must be avoided.

Optimization of the model parameter values, often used in conjunction with technical indicators, can only be useful if the model generates acceptable results for a wide range of values. I strongly recommend that the number of parameters that can be varied be kept to a bare minimum. The minimum number depends on the model logic, but usually more than two variable parameters in a single model can result in "over-fitting."

Another way to approach model improvement is to separate the logic used to generate entry points and concentrate on improving the logic of generating the corresponding exit points. In this way, the effect of the model improvement process on the core model structure is minimal. However, so are the chances of a major improvement!

If any changes are made to the model in order to improve its performance, then the steps of simulation must be repeated, as shown in figure 5-4.

Chapter Six

Modeling and Simulation Example

This chapter considers an example of a simple trading model. The procedure described in chapter 5 will be followed in order to illustrate its practical use.

Model construction:

In this step the trading model under consideration is described in simple language. The model is intended for trading T-Bond Futures contracts. The process that generates the entry points is as follows:

If the close of today is higher in value than the moving average of the last two days' highs then buy one contract on the close of the day.

The process that generates the exit points is:

Exit all open long positions at the close of the next day.

Modeling:

In this step we describe the model in a way that can be implemented in the computer. In order to do this the model logic must be described in mathematical terms.

Let us consider the following parameters:

$C(0)$ = close of today;
$H(0)$ = high of today;
$H(1)$ = high of yesterday;

Then the model entry signal trigger is given by:

If $C(0) > (H(0)+H(1))/2$ then establish a long position;

The model exit signal trigger is simply the close of the next day following the day that the entry point is established:

If system in an open position then exit at $C(0)$.

The model is shown in block diagram form in figure 6-1. The input to the model is the history of prices for the close of today $C(0)$, high of today $H(0)$ and high of yesterday $H(1)$. In the case of historical testing, these input prices must be available for each date in the desired historical time span. During actual model operation, and for the purpose of trading, the input prices are needed only for the current date. In either case, the model generates an entry signal if the corresponding entry condition is true. If a position is in effect, then the model exits at the close of the current date.

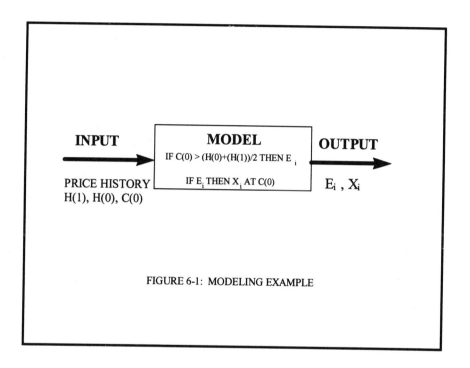

FIGURE 6-1: MODELING EXAMPLE

Implementation:

To implement our model for back testing, we can write a program in a programming language or use a software package that allows trading system model implementation and testing. Here, by the kind permission of Omega Research Inc., we are using Easy Language. The implementation in this high-level language is extremely simple and is as follows:

41

For the entry part,

IF C > AVERAGE(H,2) THEN
BUY TODAY ON THE CLOSE;

For the exit part,

EXIT TODAY ON THE CLOSE;

Easy Language does everything else automatically. It has built-in formulas for the moving average; it indexes the data properly, assigns the proper values to the variables and keeps track of open positions in order to know when to check for exit conditions. Those are just some of the many features of the software packages developed by Omega Research, Inc. that implement Easy Language.

Simulation:

In order to simulate the historical performance of this trading model I use continuously adjusted historical data of T-Bond futures for the period of 1/1/88 to 12/1/98. Commission is set at $18 round turn. The results are shown in Figure 6-2. The output provides a set of parameter values that can be used to analyze the model's historical performance. We may notice the low profitability of 49% and the small profit over the period of almost 11 years of only $14,741.25. Although the profitability is below 50%, more trades are losers than winners. The model is profitable because the ratio of average winning trade to average losing trade is 1.24, meaning that on average the system makes 1.24 times more in every winning trade than what it loses in every losing trade.

```
HISTORICAL RESULTS : Performance Summary                    Model : EXAMPLE
Trades   Equity   Chart   Highlights   View-model   Options
Summary, Detailed, Listing

========================= US          12/99 - All trades =========
 Test #      1 of    1                       Space bar to toggle display

 Total net profit            $14,741.25
 Gross profit                $91,074.25  Gross loss              $-76,333.00

 Total # of trades                 405  Percent profitable             49%
 Number winning trades             199  Number losing trades           206

 Largest winning trade        $1,669.50 Largest losing trade     $-1,580.50
 Average winning trade          $457.66 Average losing trade     $ -370.55
 Ratio avg win/avg loss           1.24  Avg trade (win & loss)       $36.40

 Max consecutive winners            7   Max consecutive losers           8
 Avg # bars in winners              1   Avg # bars in losers             1

 Max closed-out drawdown      $-9,760.75 Max intra-day drawdown   $-9,760.75
 Profit factor                    1.19  Max # of contracts held          1
 Account size required        $12,760.75 Return on account            115%

= System Writer Plus ======== Omega Research, Inc. ======== Copyright 1989 =
```

Figure 6-2: Historical Performance Results

Reprinted with permission of Omega Research, Inc.

Figure 6-3 shows a graph of the trading system quarterly returns. These returns are calculated based on a $20,000 initial trading capital per contract traded, and do not include any interest or re-investment of profits. The graph helps in noticing

43

which years have bad performance and also in spotting consecutive quarterly losses.

In the example, years '88, '89, '94 and '97 show negative performance, with year '94 being the worst performer. This visual information can be valuable in the study of the performance of any trading system model. It is also very easy to generate using a spreadsheet or a statistical analysis software package.

Model Verification and Validation:

The first priority is to verify the correct operation of the implemented model. Starting from the logic that generates the exit points, the developer must verify that trades last one trading day maximum; i.e., the model exits all trades at the close of the next day of the trade input. Looking over entry and exit dates can easily accomplish this. If a trade is found that lasts more than one day then there is something wrong with the programming implementation.

The entry logic can be verified by randomly choosing a few entry points generated by the model, and performing the calculation for the condition listed in the Modeling step. In this case that task is easy, since the two highs of the last two days must be added, the result divided by two, and compared to the last day's close. With Easy Language, and for the purpose of this simple trading system, if the developer has chosen the right function to calculate the moving average, this step is not really necessary. If the developer has chosen to write a computer program for the simulation, then this step is highly recommended.

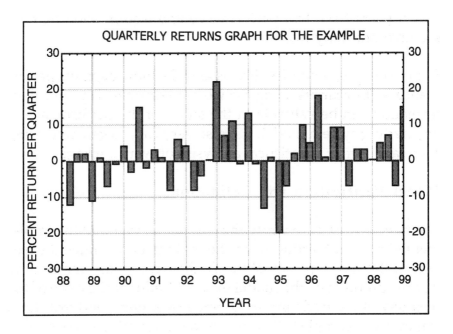

Figure 6-3: Graph of Quarterly Returns

Interpretation of the Results:

The results obtained seem to indicate a poorly performing trading system. The low profitability in conjunction with the low ratio of average win to average loss is undesirable. However, the presence of the high number of trades, 37 per year on average, leaves some room for possible model improvement, and that is what will be attempted next. Furthermore, the results from the inspection of Figure 6-3 suggest improvement of the quarterly returns for the years with negative performance. Therefore, the developer may look at ways of reducing the trading losses while, at the same time, increasing the gains.

Model Improvement:

Without adding any new variables to the model, I will attempt to improve its performance by improving the exit signal part. Thus, I will abandon the exit signal used and will incorporate a profit target and protective stop loss into the model. In Easy Language that can be done in a very simple way and all the necessary checking is done by the program.

A profit target of a full point and a half (48 ticks) and a protective stop of a full point (32 ticks) is applied. The simulation result is shown in Figure 6-4. The profitability of the model is now above 50% and the total profit has increased significantly. However, that was done at the expense of higher drawdown. The drawdown is higher in year '94 where the model now suffers greater losses. This is shown on Figure 6-5, a graph of the quarterly returns of the new model. Although years '88, '89 and '97 have now turned to positive performance, the loss for year '94 is higher. Therefore, one thing was gained at the expense of another.

Please note that the best use of the graphs showing the quarterly performance is to study individual performance and not to make relative comparisons on the magnitudes of the quarterly returns. This is true since both graphs are calculated based on a $20,000 initial trading capital but the two models have different account size requirements. Comparisons of return magnitudes may require proper adjustments to be made in the initial trading capital of the second system to reflect the higher drawdown presence.

```
HISTORICAL RESULTS : Performance Summary                    Model : EXAMPLE
Trades   Equity   Chart   Highlights   View-model   Options
Summary, Detailed, Listing

══════════════ US              12/99 - All trades ═══════════
 Test #      1 of    1                     Space bar to toggle display

 Total net profit          $63,271.00
 Gross profit             $175,282.25  Gross loss              -112,011.25

 Total # of trades             228     Percent profitable          51%
 Number winning trades         118     Number losing trades        110

 Largest winning trade     $1,888.25   Largest losing trade     $-1,049.25
 Average winning trade     $1,485.44   Average losing trade     $-1,018.28
 Ratio avg win/avg loss        1.46    Avg trade (win & loss)     $277.50

 Max consecutive winners        8      Max consecutive losers        6
 Avg # bars in winners          6      Avg # bars in losers          4

 Max closed-out drawdown   $-13,968.00 Max intra-day drawdown  $-14,655.50
 Profit factor                 1.56    Max # of contracts held       1
 Account size required     $17,655.50  Return on account           358%

═ System Writer Plus ═════════ Omega Research, Inc. ═════════ Copyright 1989 ═
```

Figure 6-4: Historical Performance of Improved Model

Reprinted with permission of Omega Research, Inc.

The new simulation results also indicate that the number of trades has been cut almost in half. The reason for this is the new exit logic which causes the trade duration to be longer, an average of 6 days for the winners and 4 days for the losers, as compared to the original model where trades last only one day. Therefore, there are now entry points that are triggered but are not taken into consideration because a long position is already in place. That is the way the testing software package used operates. There are other software packages that allow position accumulation, if that is the intention of the developer.

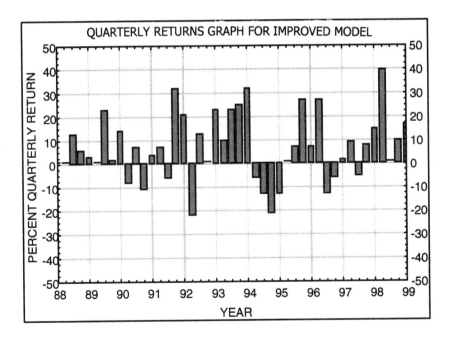

Figure 6-5. Graph of Quarterly Returns of Improved Model

The developer must repeat the Verification and Validation steps for the modified model. Then model improvement can be considered again, unless the developer decides to use or abandon the model.

Whether this example of a trading system model can be accepted and applied in real-life trading depends on the trading objectives set. Different developers may have different criteria for accepting or rejecting trading system performance. This area is as subjective as it can be. Furthermore, the trading system example was presented here for educational purposes only.

Summary

The basic concepts behind trading system modeling and simulation were illustrated with the use of an example. Development of a winning trading system that can be used under real trading conditions to result in long-term consistent profitability is a very difficult task that requires hard work and discipline. As a developer spends more time and effort towards this goal, the chances of achieving it improve accordingly. Luck seems to play no role here.

The use of software packages that facilitate trading system implementation and testing can significantly speed up the development process. This gain comes at the expense of the knowledge of the inner workings of these packages. In my experience, anything of significance that can provide a competitive advantage to the user must be developed from ground zero. In this way, the developer comes to possess an intimate understanding of his system.

SECTION TWO

TRADING

WITH

SHORT-TERM PRICE PATTERNS

Background

The most important ability that a trading system model must have, in order to be used successfully under short-term trading conditions, is to time market moves. Historical price patterns seem to perform well in that respect. They can provide an indication of the direction of prices with a high-probability success rate. I noticed that in the late 80's, after I spent considerable time and effort testing the performance of trading models using traditional technical indicators and formulas. By that time I was convinced that the only way to long-term profitability was to trade short term with a mechanical trading system. That started my search for a more effective approach to short-term trading.

During the endless hours that I was spending testing trading systems then, I also noticed that historical price patterns could be grouped together to form a short-term trading system that had very appealing performance characteristics. The problem was finding a sufficient number of patterns to put together in a trading system model. That, combined with the slow processor speeds available at the time, made the task of implementing and testing such a trading model very difficult and time-consuming. Nevertheless, during that period I used a search technique based on a visual inspection of historical price charts, followed by historical testing by writing code in Basic programming language.

The arrival of Easy Language by Omega Research, Inc. was a relief, as far as testing was concerned. However, the problem of uncovering profitable patterns from historical price data remained. Nevertheless, I managed to find a reasonable number

53

of patterns in a period of two years, and I developed my first short-term trading system. I used that system to trade T-Bond futures contracts with very satisfactory results. In 1994, I joined the World Cup Championship of Futures Trading, which is organized and run by Robbins Trading Company, a Chicago-based brokerage firm, and by the end of the year I finished in fourth place. That was a contest with real money and actual trading that lasted all year long. The good performance results of my short-term trading system motivated me to look for new ways to discover short-term price patterns. That led to the development of an automated system that can be used to search for price patterns. Later, after noticing some special properties of price patterns, I developed the p-Indicator. This technical indicator is based on price patterns and can be used to trade short term.

My research and development efforts, as of the writing of this book, are still in full effect. I strongly believe that the moment one abandons the effort of developing something new and better, it is the beginning of a decline to come. Regardless of what has been achieved in the past, there will always be something better to look forward to. And always someone who is searching for it...

Chapter Seven

Developing a Trading System

The Development Steps

In order to develop a short-term trading system based on historical price patterns, I first select a market to trade—for instance, the T-Bond Futures at CBOT. I obtain historical price charts, print them out and then start to work my way into discovering patterns. The patterns I search for have a simple form, which is based on the open, high, low and close of daily bars. I try to look as far back as ten days, but that can be hard. Up to five days of pattern length is a reasonable objective with the visual search.

Figure 7-1 shows the development procedure followed. That may serve as a methodology for short-term trading system development, providing a systematic framework that keeps the developer in focus. The steps are as follows:

Identify Pattern:

The pattern identification is manual and is based on a visual inspection of the historical price charts. I concentrate on chart formations that generate a timely move of more than two full points in the price of the T-Bond Futures contract. When I spot a chart formation that seems to satisfy these requirements, I isolate it from the rest of the chart and draw it on a blank piece of paper. Then I attempt to identify the logic for its implementation.

Implementation:

The pattern logic is implemented in Easy Language. That speeds the implementation and, subsequently, the testing process significantly.

The problem with implementation is to decide which of the pattern characteristics need to be included. That is a trial and error process that results in a continuous feedback loop between the implementation and the simulation steps. There is no recipe for doing this besides the trial and error way. It is just time-consuming.

Simulation:

A trading system model based on a single pattern is tested on historical price data of the T-Bond Futures contract, going back to the beginning of the price history. The following values for the performance parameters are desired:

Percent Profitability: > 67%

Number of Trades: > 20
Maximum Number of Consecutive Losers: < 4

A profit target and protective stop, each a full point in magnitude, are used in testing. That is equal to 32 ticks of movement, or $1,000, per contract traded in the T-Bonds. These values are selected as optimum and that was the result of a historical volatility study aimed at maximizing short-term move size while minimizing the duration of a trade. The trade-off comes from the fact that the higher the profit target or stop, the longer the system remains in a position. At the same time, low values for the stop loss take the system out of the position too soon. High values of the stop loss also subject the system to wide equity variations.

Whether a particular pattern is accepted or rejected depends upon the performance parameter values. When the number of trades appears to be small, the pattern logic is simplified and tested again. Most often that results in a degradation of the performance, but at times the result is better. The process is repeated with several variations of the logic and the best performance is selected, if any is acceptable. If none is acceptable, the pattern is discarded.

Add to Model:

Short-term price patterns with desirable performance characteristics are added to a model that is made up of individual pattern units. The model is implemented in Easy Language and individual patterns are allowed to interact; that is, if the model is in a long position, a pattern that generates short positions can become active, closing out that long position before a target or stop are hit, while also establishing a new short position. Easy Language allows that in a simple way, using global variables.

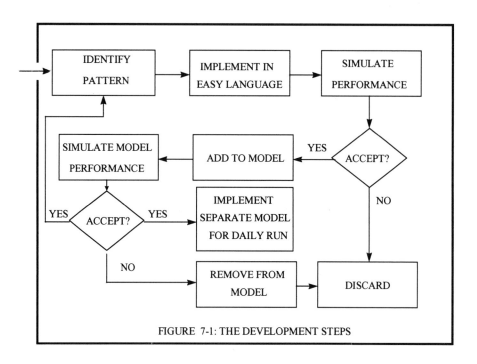

FIGURE 7-1: THE DEVELOPMENT STEPS

Simulate Model Performance:

Each time a new pattern is added, the resulting new trading system is tested to simulate its performance under historical price conditions, as well as to examine the result of the interaction of the new pattern with the model made up of the previously selected patterns. Besides the overall performance characteristics, I pay attention to the increase in the number of trades of the new model, as compared with the trades of the individual new pattern. If there is no change in the total number of trades, this may mean that the new pattern is redundant. A satisfactory increase in the total number of trades would be in the vicinity of 50% of the number of trades generated by the newly implemented pattern alone. The *interaction ratio* is defined as the total number of trades of the combined pattern model divided by the sum of the individual trades generated by each pattern separately. The final result for that ratio in the first model I developed was 0.7 (i.e., individual patterns interacted 30% of the time), and I accept that to be a satisfactory ratio for my purposes.

If the new pattern added is considered redundant or affects the interaction to the extent that either the profitability is reduced or the drawdown is increased to an unacceptable level, then that pattern is removed from the model and discarded.

The pattern search then continues and the steps are repeated for each new pattern found. I stop when I think that a model with satisfactory performance characteristics has been developed. The trading system model I developed back in the early 90's had 30 patterns that could generate long entry signals and 25 that could generate short entry signals. That gave me at least one entry signal, or trade, every week, on the average.

Implement Separate Model for Daily Run:

Every new pattern that is found which satisfies the desired performance criteria is first added to the pattern collection that forms the short-term trading system model, and then a separate trading model is implemented for just that single pattern. The objective of the separate model is to assist in daily signal generation and trading.

Daily Model Operation

When a trading system model suitable for short-term trading is available, the goal is to use it in a systematic way to generate trading signals and trading profits. As much as someone may wish that after the completion of the model development task the goal of becoming a successful trader is accomplished, nothing could be further than the truth! The real work starts when a good trading model is available. The object is to have a methodology and procedure in place that will fit the particular trading style of the trader and impose a discipline that will minimize actions that fall outside the scope or operation of the model.

In the trading model made from a collection of short-term patterns, some of the entry signals initiate a position at the open of the next day, but most do it at the close of the day that the pattern formation is completed. The latter could not be avoided since experience has shown that the close of the day, as a position entry point, is very important in some pattern formations because it is a strong indication of short-term market direction and price momentum.

Therefore, the intention is to generate a comprehensive daily trading plan that would list the position status of all patterns and assist the trader in placing orders for those patterns that become valid on a particular day. The trader must know in advance which patterns have a possibility to become active and then prepare for position entry. This implies that the conditions that could potentially make those patterns valid are available to the trader in a presentable form.

The methodology for the daily operation of the trading system is shown in Figure 7-2. The steps followed are:

Update Database

An end-of day data service is used to update the database file of the daily prices of the T-Bond futures contract. Most data services have proprietary format but provide a software package that allows converting the data to other popular formats, including ASCII, which was used here.

Run All Models in Daily Mode

This is done to determine the position status of each individual model representing each pattern in the short-term trading system model developed. If any of the individual models has a position status, long or short, that is noted in the output of the system. In the past, I used the "Autorun" feature of System Writer Plus, an Omega Research, Inc. product. That was very convenient, since the model logic was already written in Easy Language, which was a part of that software package. It also served as a way to check and validate the results of the daily report and to correct any programming errors that might have been present.

Generate Daily Report for the Trader

Some of the individual patterns in the model generate entry signals at the open of the next day, but most do that at the close of the day that the pattern is formed. For the latter, in order for the trader to be able to act when the pattern is formed and a position must be placed, there is a need to determine in advance the progression of the formation. Because of the number of patterns involved, this must be done in a way that is easy for the trader to monitor. One way to predict the formation's progression is to determine which patterns are candidates to give a signal at the close of the next trading day and to list the necessary conditions that must be satisfied for that purpose. I call this the "next day projection technique." Chapter 10 describes this technique in greater detail.

For each individual pattern model, additional code is written to facilitate next-day projection. That generates an output for each pattern that is a candidate to produce an entry signal, and all the outputs are combined to form a daily report file. The file is then printed out and is available to the trader as the next day's trading plan.

Monitor Prices

During the trading day, the trader monitors market prices and checks the various conditions listed on the daily report. If there is a price move that invalidates a listed condition for a particular pattern, the trader then crosses that pattern out and no longer considers it a candidate to produce a trading entry signal by the close of the day. As the trading day progresses, more patterns are invalidated. Usually, as the market close gets near, there is a small number of candidate patterns to produce a signal.

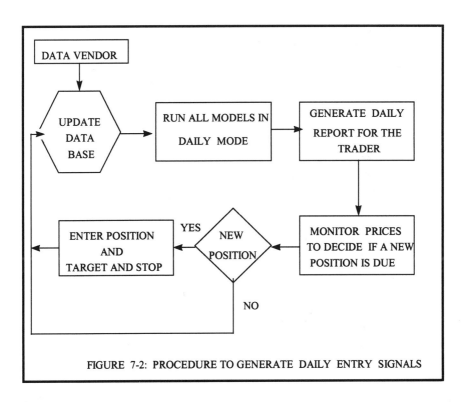

FIGURE 7-2: PROCEDURE TO GENERATE DAILY ENTRY SIGNALS

Position Entering:

If the prices move in a way as to trigger a particular pattern then the trader inputs the appropriate order. When the order is executed, a profit target and a stop loss order are also put in place as a "good 'til canceled" order. Since the profit target and the stop loss are two full points apart, the order is taken at the CBOT pit on a "non-held basis." If the movement of prices is such that the trader cannot determine with absolute certainty that a position is due, then that pattern is reconsidered after a market close. If an entry signal is triggered then, the trader enters the position in the evening session. This may result in some slippage, but in practice the long-term variations usually average out to zero.

In the case that the trading model has an open position in the market, long or short, and another entry signal is generated that is of the same direction, then the new signal is neglected. However, the trader may use the indication of that signal as a confirmation of the position in place or may decide to move the original position stops to new levels, as if the new entry has been put in place. There are many ways to treat multiple signals and consecutive signals, depending on the money management objectives of the trader. The possibilities are many and have yet to be explored.

An Example

An example of a pattern formation is shown in figure 7-3. The three daily bars that form the pattern have been labeled, starting from 0 for the last day or today, 1 for yesterday and 2 for two days ago. The pattern logic is as follows:

Buy today on the close if

Close of yesterday < Low of two days ago   and
Low of yesterday < Low of today   and
Close of today > High of two days ago   and
Close of today > Open of today;

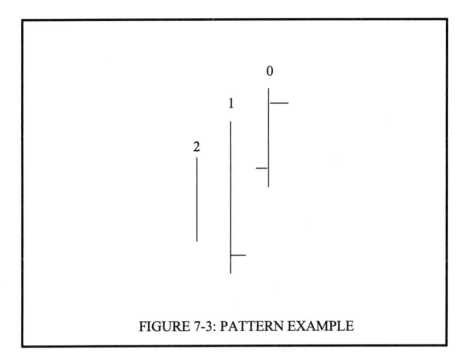

FIGURE 7-3: PATTERN EXAMPLE

The Easy Language implementation for this pattern, for both testing and daily operation, is shown in Figure 7-4. The code written has two portions. The first is the portion used to check the pattern logic conditions. If the conditions are all true then the program checks to determine whether the end of the data file, containing the T-Bond daily price data, has been reached. The end of the file is the last trading bar available. If the last bar has been reached then the system initiates a position, as well as a profit target and stop loss. It also prints out the daily report—the status of the signal.

```
Directory : C:\L3                 Printed on   : 02/17/98 04:49pm

                   ENTRY SIGNAL

Signal Name    : H&D RT LONG           Developer   : HARRIS
Notes : HD SYSTEM
Last Update : 02/17/98 04:47pm
Long  Entry Verified : YES

/////////////////////////////////// LONG ENTRY
\\\\\\\\\\\\\\\\\\\\\\\\\\\\\\\\\\

condition1=c(1) < l(2);
condition2=l(1) < l(0);
condition3=c(0) > o(0);
condition4=c(0) > h(2);
IF condition1 and condition2 and condition3 and condition4
THEN BEGIN
IF DATE=LASTCALCDATE THEN
PRINT(FILE1,"H&D:        LONG - EXIT AT ENTRY PRICE + 32 TICKS");
BUY TODAY GVALUE1 CONTRACTS ON THE CLOSE WITH BEGIN
PROFIT TARGET AT CLOSE OF TODAY + GVALUE32 POINTS;
PROTECTIVE STOP AT CLOSE OF TODAY - GVALUE32 POINTS;
END;
END
ELSE BEGIN
IF DATE = LASTCALCDATE AND C(0) < L(1) THEN BEGIN
VALUE1=H(1);
VALUE2=INTPORTION(VALUE1);
VALUE3=INTPORTION(FRACPORTION(VALUE1)*32+0.5);
VALUE4=L(0);
VALUE5=INTPORTION(VALUE4);
VALUE6=INTPORTION(FRACPORTION(VALUE4)*32+0.5);
PRINT(FILE1,"H&D: FLAT, CLOSE >",VALUE2:3:0,VALUE3:2:0,
         " CLOSE >OPEN");
PRINT(FILE1," LOW >",VALUE5:3:0,VALUE6:2:0);
END;
END;

\\\\\\\\\\\\\\\\\\\\\\\\\\\\\\\\\\\\\\\\\\\\\\//////////////////////////////////
////
Prepared using System Writer Plus Version 2.18 by Omega Research, Inc.
```

Figure 7-4: Code for the Pattern Example

The second portion of the code is used when the end of the file has been reached but not all the conditions are true. This helps to generate the daily report, in case the pattern is a candidate to generate an entry signal at the close of the next daily bar. In order to achieve this one must check to see if the actual daily bar formations are such to allow an entry signal. That can only be true if, for the bars labeled 1 and 2 in the pattern formation, their associated conditions are met by the last two bars in the data. Then we must shift the labels of the bars to be compatible with those of the code, as shown in figure 7-5. Thus, bar 1 becomes bar 0 and bar 2 becomes bar 1. Since there is only one condition that involves the original bars 1 and 2, we check to see whether or not this is true—but only if the end of file has been reached. If the condition is true, then the values for the rest of the conditions are printed to a file. The three conditions that must be met on the next day are now properly determined. Since the ASCII T-Bond daily data files are in decimal form, proper adjustments are made to print the values out in 32nds.

The testing results for this pattern are shown in figure 7-6. The testing period is from 01/01/86 to 01/01/98. A commission of $14 was used in the testing.

In figure 7-7, a daily trading report as of the close of 02/19/98 is shown. In this report, patterns that generate long positions are listed first, followed by patterns that generate short positions. Each pattern that is a candidate to generate a trading signal at the close of the next day is listed and has been assigned a name for clarity. Of course, the trading system includes additional patterns that are not candidates to generate a signal as of the close of the particular day the report is generated, none of which are listed here. Furthermore, the daily report may look quite different each day, since the particular patterns that are candidates to generate a signal constantly change.

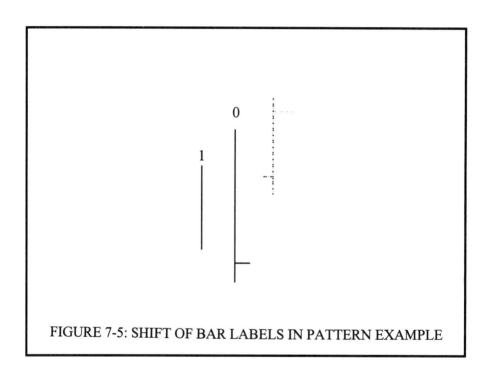

FIGURE 7-5: SHIFT OF BAR LABELS IN PATTERN EXAMPLE

The conditions shown for the next day—open, high, low and close—are part of each pattern's logic. For example, the pattern named RECOVER, in the Long Signal part of the report, will generate a long position signal if the close of the next day in the T-Bond future contract is higher than 122 17/32 and the low during the day session remains above 122 1/32. If during the trading day the low drops below 122 1/32, let us say to a price of 121 19/32, then the particular signal is crossed out and invalidated, even if the condition for the close is valid.

```
HISTORICAL RESULTS : Performance Summary          Model : H&D LONG RT
 Trades   Equity   Chart   Highlights   View-model   Options
Summary, Detailed, Listing
═══════════════ US              12/99 - All trades ═══════════
 Test #      1 of    1                    Space bar to toggle display

 Total net profit          $9,692.00
 Gross profit             $15,776.00  Gross loss              $-6,084.00

 Total # of trades            22     Percent profitable           72%
 Number winning trades        16     Number losing trades          6

 Largest winning trade     $986.00   Largest losing trade    $-1,014.00
 Average winning trade     $986.00   Average losing trade    $-1,014.00
 Ratio avg win/avg loss      0.97    Avg trade (win & loss)     $440.55

 Max consecutive winners      6      Max consecutive losers        3
 Avg # bars in winners        4      Avg # bars in losers          4

 Max closed-out drawdown  $-3,070.00 Max intra-day drawdown   $-3,510.75
 Profit factor               2.59    Max # of contracts held       1
 Account size required    $5,510.75  Return on account           175%
═ System Writer Plus ═════ Omega Research, Inc. ═════ Copyright 1989 ═
```

Figure 7-6: Testing Results for the Pattern Example

Reprinted with permission of Omega Research, Inc.

DATE: 980218

	INCLUDING EVENING	DAY ONLY
CLOSE:	122 1	122 1
OPEN:	122 19	122 19
HIGH:	122 26	122 26
LOW:	121 30	121 30

REAL TIME CALCULATION RESULTS FOR T-BOND TRADING SYSTEM

CONTRACT SIZE: $100,000 - MINIMUM MOVE: 0.03125 = $31.25 = 1/32 = 1 TICK TARGET/STOP: 32 TICKS = $1,000

LONG SIGNALS: POSITION   CONDITIONS TO ENTER A LONG POSITION

BOTTOM: FLAT,   LOW OF DAY < 122 3 LOW OF DAY > 121 29
CLOSE > 122 23

REVERSE: FLAT,   OPEN < 121 30 LOW < 122 1
CLOSE > 122 26

RECOVER: FLAT,   CLOSE > 122 17 LOW OF DAY > 122 1

REVERSAL: FLAT,   CLOSE > 122 26 OPEN > 122 1 OPEN < 122 19
LOW > 121 30 LOW < 122 1

COVERUP: FLAT,   CLOSE > 122 26 OPEN < 121 30

SHORT SIGNALS: POSITION   CONDITIONS TO ENTER A SHORT POSITION

REVERSE: FLAT,   OPEN > 122 26 HIGH > 122 1 CLOSE > 121 16

SLIDE: FLAT,   HIGH > 123 0 CLOSE > 120 29

INSIDE: FLAT,   HIGH < 122 26 LOW > 121 30 CLOSE < OPEN
CLOSE < 121 29

UNDER: FLAT,   HIGH < 122 26 LOW < 121 30 CLOSE < 121 17
OPEN > CLOSE

SPIRAL: FLAT,   CLOSE < 121 15

Figure 7-7: Daily Report Generation

Occasionally the trading system may generate both a long and a short position. That has happened only a handful of times in the past. In such cases, no position is taken. Conversely, the more signals that become valid at the close,
the better the chances may be for that position to produce a profit. Chapter 12 will discuss, in greater detail, some interesting aspects of trading models that are made up of price patterns.

Summary

This chapter presented a detailed methodology that can be used to develop short-term trading systems based on historical price patterns and apply them in actual trading. Successful application of the methodology requires hard work on the part of the developer because it involves a manual search of historical price data and extensive trial-and-error testing. It also requires discipline on the part of the trader to monitor and execute a detailed daily trading plan. Doing both properly results in a systematic trading methodology that can be very rewarding.

Chapter Eight

Short-term Price Patterns

In this book, a *pattern* is defined as a chart formation that is made up of consecutive price bars. The bars can have any time period length. Patterns can only be compared in the sense of the algorithm used to describe them. Those patterns that have multiple occurrences that look alike visually are just special cases in the vast universe of abstract mathematical pattern forms. Therefore, if one intends to perform a systematic search for patterns, it may be helpful to have a basic classification that accounts for different types. Here I attempt to present a non-exhaustive list of the types of patterns that one may consider in a search.

Exact:

These are the most common and easy-to-understand patterns. They are "exact" because every occurrence matches the other occurrences of the same pattern 100%, in the sense of an algorithm. These types of patterns are also easy to compare visually, since their geometric form is very consistent; i.e., all the occurrences of the same pattern look alike in a geometrical sense.

However, proportions are not kept to ratio—only the relative positions of price bars in the chart formation are kept constant. Figure 8-1 shows an example of two occurrences of an Exact pattern. The pattern is made up of five price bars. Note that the relative position of all bars in each of the two occurrences is the same. However, bar 3 in the first occurrence is bigger than the corresponding bar 3' of the second occurrence. Also, the positions of the open and close of bar 2 are different than those of the corresponding bar 2'. Despite these differences, the two occurrences may look alike to the untrained eye.

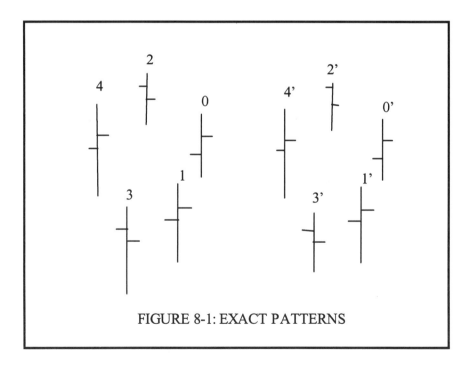

FIGURE 8-1: EXACT PATTERNS

Matched:

These patterns are matched to a desired "matching level" expressed as a percentage. Again, that is true only in the sense of the algorithm used; i.e., the matching is a mathematical comparison and occurrences of the same pattern may not look alike visually at all. The degree of matching can be selected arbitrarily, but levels above 50% are needed to produce desirable results. A matching level of 100% results in an "Exact" type pattern, by definition.

Matched patterns can be thought of as sets that are formed by the union of subsets of Exact patterns. The patterns of each subset "match" the patterns of the other subsets at the desired matching level or higher. Each subset defines a distinct Exact pattern with its own number of occurrences in history. The limiting case is when each subset has only one occurrence and matches the rest at a 100% level, which is the definition of an Exact pattern. In that case the number of subsets also coincides with the number of occurrences of the Exact pattern.

Figure 8-2 illustrates the concept of a matched pattern by showing two different Exact patterns. Each of the Exact patterns belongs to a subset and has a given number of historical occurrences. The union of the subsets forms the matched pattern set. A close inspection can show that the two patterns resemble each other greatly but are not quite the same.

Proportional:

These are patterns where every occurrence of the same pattern exhibits the same proportions in terms of daily ranges, expressed as the distance between the High and the Low of every corresponding bar. That is, the ratio of the first bar range to the second bar range is the same in all occurrences. The same holds for the ratio of the second bar to the third, the ratio of the third to the forth, and so on. The motivation in searching for this type of pattern is to look for geometric symmetry that is often hidden in seemingly random data.

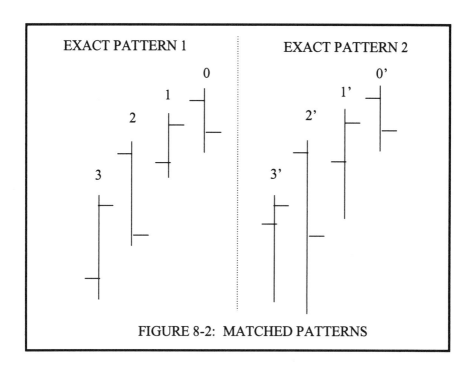

FIGURE 8-2: MATCHED PATTERNS

Delay:

These are patterns that can be of any type, but order entry occurs with a delay. With delay patterns, instead of entering a position at the close of the day that the pattern is formed or at the open of the next day, the entry is taken after a number of days, called the "delay." The delay period can be several days long, depending on the pattern found by a search algorithm. The motivation in searching for this type of pattern comes from the fact that some otherwise profitable pattern formations, indicating a position to be taken in a certain direction, suffer an immediate correction due to profit taking. The delay used allows a trader to filter out the correction and take a position when the market resumes direction.

Figure 8-3 shows the formation of a delay pattern. The actual pattern is made up of the three bars labeled 3, 4 and 5. The rest of the bars, 2, 1 and 0 are shown with dotted lines indicating that their relative position on the chart is of no importance to the pattern formation. Position initiation, whether that is a long or short, occurs at the open or close of bar 0. Note that the delay period is the same for all occurrences of the same pattern.

Split:

These are patterns that are compositions of different but consecutive patterns types, a first and a second, in the simplest case. Every occurrence of the same Split pattern has identical corresponding parts, whether they are of the Exact, Matched, Proportional or, in the case of the second pattern, Delay type. In addition, the two parts must be in the same order in the Split pattern formation of all occurrences. When comparing Split patterns, an algorithm should match each of the two parts, or two patterns, separately.

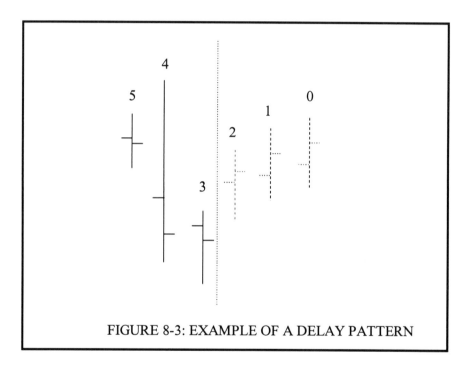

FIGURE 8-3: EXAMPLE OF A DELAY PATTERN

The motivation in searching for Split patterns is twofold: first, to allow for patterns that have a greater number of days in their formation, since the splitting into two parts greatly reduces the number of conditions that an algorithm must match and therefore increases the number of occurrences; second, to increase the probability of success, since the second pattern can be used as a confirmation to the first pattern's indication for a position entry in a certain direction, long or short.

In the case of a Split pattern made up of Matched pattern types, each part of the Split pattern is matched to a desired matching level. Usually the last part of the split pattern is matched to a higher level than the first, as it is the final formation before taking a position.

Inter-Market:

These can be patterns of any type that appear in the data of one contract, but indicate a position to be taken on another contract. For instance, a pattern can be found that, when formed in S&P 500 Index futures price chart, indicates taking a position in T-Bond futures. The results can be quite interesting when searching for such patterns. The motivation for this type of search is the apparent interdependence of some markets, as market players keep shifting assets from one market to the other depending on prevailing economic conditions.

In order to more clearly describe the different pattern types, let us make the following definitions.

Let **P** be defined as a pattern of the following types:

E: Exact
M_k: Matched, k = the matching level in percent
PR_n: Proportional, n = proportionality ratio

Let us also define the following operators on the above pattern types:

S: Split
D_j: Delay, $j = 1,2,3,\ldots,n$ the delay in bars
IM: Inter-Market

We can use the definitions above to describe pattern types. For instance, an exact pattern is defined as follows:

$P=\{E\}$
and a matched pattern as:

$P = \{M_{80}\}$, with matching level of 80%

Please note that $\{M_{100}\} = \{E\}$, by definition.

A proportional pattern with 75% proportionality ratio is described as:

$P = \{PR_{75}\}$

We can also use the operators defined above to describe more complicated pattern types:

A split pattern is defined as follows:

$P = S\{P_1, P_2\}$, and it is formed by linking each of the two patterns, one right after the other. The patterns, P_1 and P_2, can be of any type.

A delay pattern is defined as:

$P = D\{P_1\}$, P_1 being a pattern of any type.

An inter-market pattern is defined as:

$P = IM\{P_1\}$, an inter-market pattern of any type, P_1.

Below, we illustrate the use of pattern types and operators to describe specific pattern formations:

$P_1 = D_4\{E\}$, is an exact pattern with 4 days delay.

$P_2 = D_7\{M_{95}\}$, is a pattern matched at 95% level, that has 7 days delay.

$P_3 = S\{M_{75}, E\}$, is a split pattern formed by linking two patterns, one matched at a 75% level and the other of the Exact type.

$P_4 = S\{M_{75}, M_{85}\}$, is a split-matched pattern formed by linking two matched patterns, one at 75% and the other at 85%.

$P_5 = S\{M_{90}, D_3\{PR_{75}\}\}$ is a split pattern formed by a matched pattern to the 90% level and a proportional pattern with 75% proportionality ratio and 3 day delay in taking a position.

$P_6 = IM\{S\{M_{65}, D_2\{E\}\}\}$ is an inter-market split pattern, formed by linking together a 65% matched pattern and an exact pattern with a 2 days delay.

I will omit any rigorous mathematical treatment of pattern types and operators—a topic that falls outside the scope of this book but is slated to be the subject of a future publication.

Chapter Nine

Automated Pattern Search

In chapter seven I described a procedure to develop short-term trading system models based on historical price patterns. The search for the patterns was a trial-and-error approach, which consisted of visually inspecting historical price charts and selecting possible candidates. The pattern logic was then implemented and back tested to determine whether the selected candidates satisfied a set of desired performance characteristics. This manual method is a very tedious and time-consuming procedure, the results of which depend on the patience of the developer to visually examine large volumes of historical data and guess correctly on the possible existence of patterns hidden in it.

The type of search for short-term price patterns described above raised the following questions:

• How many patterns can be out there?

• Are there patterns that are mathematical forms and cannot be discovered by a visual inspection of the charts?

• What are the maximum and minimum length, in daily bars, that patterns with acceptable performance characteristics can have?

• Which parameters should be included in the pattern implementation?

Answering these questions requires something more than a trial-and-error procedure. It requires a systematic approach to pattern searching. That is the motivation behind the idea of automating the pattern search procedure. The objective is to try to exploit computing power (which keeps getting faster and faster, while the cost continues to drop), and to let a system designed to do just that run as long as it needs to get results. A short way of conducting an exhaustive search that uses the whole history of available data to identify patterns that possess a set of desired performance criteria.

The idea may be easy to conceptualize but is very difficult to implement. A software program needed to be written that would perform the search, and this seemed like a monumental task at the time that the idea was conceived. Nevertheless, the goal was set in early 1994, and a working first version of the software was available by the end of 1995.

The Procedure

Figure 9-1 shows the procedure followed for the automatic search of short-term patterns.

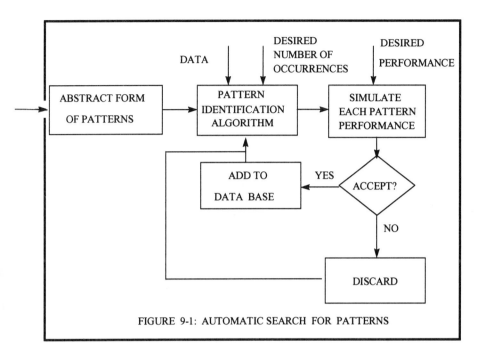

FIGURE 9-1: AUTOMATIC SEARCH FOR PATTERNS

Abstract Form of Patterns:

Chapter 8 gives an introduction to pattern types. The form, or type, of the patterns to be discovered is described here in terms of their general structure and composition of parameters. This is a general description and may vary according to the developer's objective. Such a description is necessary in order for the search algorithm to be able to compare two patterns and decide whether or not they belong in the same set. There are many different ways to approach this issue, but attention should be given to the computational complexity involved, since the search process is calculation intensive.

Pattern Identification Algorithm:

This algorithm is the "heart" of the search process. It searches the data continuously and comes up with possible candidates for patterns. The input to this algorithm is the price history of the commodity considered and the desired number of occurrences, N, of the patterns to be found:

Desired number of occurrences: $> N$

The length of the patterns considered by the search algorithm can be of several days, or bars, long.

Simulate Performance:

When the search algorithm finds a pattern that satisfies the *minimum number of occurrences* requirement, it passes the characteristics of that pattern to a module that is designed to test historical performance. That module is used to determine if the pattern found also satisfies the *minimum percent profitability* and *maximum number of consecutive losers* criteria. That is:
Percent Profitability: $> P\%$
Maximum Number of Consecutive Losers: $< C_L$

calculated based on:

Protective Stop: $= S$
Profit Target: $= G$

where the protective stop and profit target are set to the desired levels, S and G respectively. For instance, in the T-Bond future, those can each be one full point or 32 ticks. Both the close of the day that the pattern formation is complete and the open of the next day are considered in the simulation as the position entry point. The system keeps as the entry point the one that gives the best performance. If the performance is acceptable, the detailed pattern characteristics are stored in a database; otherwise it is discarded, and the search moves on. A complete search may last several days or even several weeks, depending on processor speed and length of historical input data.

Below is an example of numbers used as the input to the search and simulation algorithms:

Desired number of occurrences:	> 30
Percent Profitability:	> 67%
Maximum Number of Consecutive Losers:	< 3

As the desired number of occurrences is increased, for constant percent profitability and maximum number of consecutive losers, the probability of finding a pattern that satisfies all the criteria is decreased. To increase the probability, either the percent profitability must be reduced or the maximum number of consecutive losers increased.

Different sets of protective stops and profit targets may be selected for the search. Examples for different futures contracts are shown in table 9-1.

Contract	Profit Target (In points)	Protective Stop (In points)
T-Bonds	1 2 2	1 2 1
S&P 500	5 8 10	5 8 10
Crude Oil	0.5 1	0.5 1
S-Franc	1 1.5	1 1.5

Table 9-1: Examples of Targets and Stops

When considering a specific futures contract, the S&P 500 for instance, several search runs may be made for different sets of input criteria to the search algorithm and profit target and stop levels. One can only determine the appropriate range of magnitude for each of the parameters after completing a number of searches and an evaluation of the results generated.

Chapter Ten

Total Short-term Trading
Methodology

A complete systems trading approach must include a trading system model with good performance parameters and a methodology that facilitates model operation in a way that can be used easily by the trader on a daily basis. Patterns found by the automatic search procedure described in chapter 9 can be used in concert to form a short-term trading system. What is then needed is a methodology that will use those patterns in an effective way to generate trading signals. The procedure followed for daily operation is shown, in block diagram form, in Figure 10-1. This routine enforces a specific mode of operation, and must be executed daily by the trader. Furthermore, although general, the procedure is systematic because it provides an operational framework with rigid structure that cannot be altered during operation. It directs the trader to focus on the specific trading system execution. Of course, the ultimate responsibility to conform with the results lies with the will of the individual trader and is a matter of discipline that no system can forcefully impose on anyone.

Daily Operation

First the database of daily prices is updated for each futures contract considered, and then the following steps are observed.

Running of Daily Projections:

For each contract considered, like T-Bonds or S&P 500 Index, the patterns found by the search algorithm are stored in the data base in a form that describes each pattern's full characteristics. Then an algorithm that runs on a daily basis takes each pattern from the data base and determines whether it has a formation up to the current date that might produce an entry signal, either by the close of the next day or by the open of the day following the next trading day. The patterns that are candidates are grouped together in terms of their contract type and profit target and stop levels. The conditions that must be met in order to produce a signal are then calculated.

Daily Report:

A daily report is printed out for each contract traded and for each level of the profit target and stop. Figure 10-2 shows two examples of reports for the NYMEX Crude Oil futures. Both examples are for the Exact type patterns with zero delay. The first output is FILE cl55cl0, which denotes the contract CL (Crude Oil) with 0.5 points of profit target and 0.5 points of stop loss. The second output is FILE cl11cl0, also for Crude Oil, with one full point profit target and stop. In both cases, the patterns generate signals that initiate a position at the close of the day that the patterns are formed. The date of the daily report generation is 02/18/1998.

The daily report of each file lists first the long patterns and then the short patterns. Each pattern is identified by the date of the first day in the data file that the search algorithm noticed its occurrence. The profit target value and stop loss value are then listed—the profitability of the pattern and then the conditions that must be met on the next trading day so that the pattern generates a trading signal. Notice that the daily report lists only patterns that are candidates to generate a position as of that specific report date. There are other patterns that are not candidates because their formation up to the current date does not qualify them as such. Each day's report may be quite different from the last, in terms of the specific patterns listed.

For example, in file cl11cl0, the long pattern named 840323 will generate a long position at the close of the next trading day if the close of the market is above 16.45. This particular pattern's logic involves only values of the close for the final day of its formation.

Monitoring of Prices:

During the trading day the prices of the markets traded are monitored and the corresponding daily reports updated by crossing out candidate patterns whose conditions to generate a signal are invalidated. For instance, in file cl55cl0 and for long pattern 840202, one condition states: OPEN < 16.60.

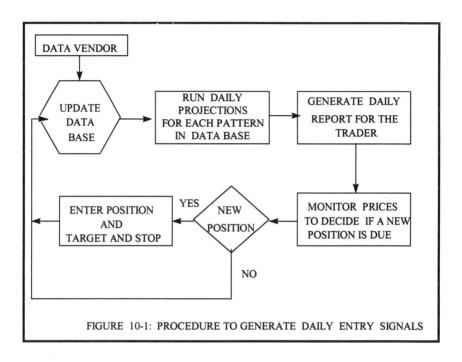

FIGURE 10-1: PROCEDURE TO GENERATE DAILY ENTRY SIGNALS

DAILY RESULTS

FILE : cl55cl0   Trade on CLOSE
DATE : 980218   DELAY : 0

DATE TRG STP PRF% C O N D I T I O N S

LONG

840202 0.50 0.50 76%   LOW < 15.68 - CLOSE > 15.68 - CLOSE <
                         OPEN. OPEN < 16.60 - HIGH > 16.60
840511 0.50 0.50 76%   OPEN = LOW - LOW < 15.68 - CLOSE >
                         15.68. CLOSE < HIGH - HIGH < 16.60

SHORT

840529 0.50 0.50 76%   LOW < CLOSE - CLOSE < 15.68 - HIGH =
                         16.45

DAILY RESULTS

FILE : CL11CL0   Trade on CLOSE
DATE : 980218   DELAY : 0

DATE TRG STP PRF% C O N D I T I O N S

LONG

840117 1.00 1.00 71% LOW < 15.68 - CLOSE > 15.68 - CLOSE < 16.45 -
                       HIGH > 16.60
840613 1.00 1.00 81% OPEN < CLOSE - CLOSE < 15.70
840323 1.00 1.00 81% CLOSE > 16.45
840126 1.00 1.00 79% LOW < 15.68 - OPEN > 15.68 - OPEN < 16.60 -
                       CLOSE > 16.60
                       CLOSE < HIGH
840202 1.00 1.00 95% LOW < 15.68 - CLOSE > 15.68 - CLOSE < OPEN -
                       OPEN < 16.60
                       HIGH > 16.60
840511 1.00 1.00 81% OPEN = LOW - LOW < 15.68 - CLOSE > 15.68 -
                       CLOSE < HIGH
                       HIGH < 16.60

SHORT

840529 1.00 1.00 81% LOW < CLOSE - CLOSE < 15.68 - HIGH = 16.45

Figure 10-2: Daily Report Example

93

If the market opens above that level, let us say at 16.65, then the pattern is no longer a candidate and is crossed out.

By the end of the trading day, as the market nears the close, most of the patterns are invalidated and crossed out.

Order Placing:

Orders are placed either at the close of the day that the pattern formation is completed or at the open of the next day. On the daily report, only the conditions for patterns that trade on the close are listed. Those that trade on the open are only listed when they are validated by the system and require a position to be placed. These, if present, are simple to trade since their status is known by the close of the trading day and the position is to be placed at the open of the next day. On the contrary, patterns that trade on the close of the day they are formed require some extra work to be implemented. The condition of pattern 840323 in file cl11cl0 in the report shown on Figure 10-2 is the simplest kind and the order could be placed as a "Stop Close Only" order. Other orders may be more difficult to place since the conditions may be alternating from valid to invalid near the close. If that is the case, then it is best to avoid any action, wait for the market close, and run the daily report for the next day after getting the price settlements. If the report indicates that a position should have been placed at the close of the previous day then that is done at the beginning of the night session, if any. If there is no night session then the trader must wait for the open of the next day and make appropriate adjustment to the profit target and stop loss.

Conceivably, the whole process of monitoring patterns and even that of placing the orders could also be automated. This can be done using some popular software modeling and simulation packages available to traders, which also allow operation with a real-time data feed. When doing this, however, one must be careful in the sense of what is intended to be accomplished. Although such automation may sound appealing and may solve some problems related to the amount of work needed in tracking the operation of a mechanical trading system, it is my personal view that this level of automation can alienate the trader. Furthermore, full automation may result in a lack of intimate understanding of the process that generates the trades. I have noticed several times in the past that traders who use automated trading systems often ignore the signals generated. Those traders spend their trading day watching the market prices change on the screen, instead of doing any work on their system, and thus they form an opinion about future market direction. This opinion, which is often contrary to that of their system, is the major cause of ignoring the trading signals generated by their automated mechanical system. Of course, the use of full automation is a debatable subject and others may have a different viewpoint. Furthermore, depending on a trader's previous experience and use of mechanical trading systems, various levels of automation may be implemented. Nevertheless, if full automation is implemented, it is advisable to also run in parallel a manual check of the results, at least for a good period of time. This manual check is needed in order to verify and validate the automated system's trade generation process. Avoiding this step may result in faulty operation due to programming errors that are not immediately noticeable, and consequently to wrong trade entries and, most probably, money losses.

Daily Price Projections

Price patterns which generate trading signals that initiate a position at the close of the day that they are formed, such as the examples in figure 10-2, require special handling in order to know in advance the conditions under which they will become active. I call this the "Next Day Projection Technique." As an illustration, let us consider the pattern example of chapter 7, for which the Easy Language code is shown in Figure 7-4. The conditions that must be met in order to generate a long position entry signal are:

$C(1) < L(2)$ and
$L(1) < L(0)$ and
$C(0) > O(0)$ and
$C(0) > H(2)$

where the index 0 denotes today, 1 yesterday and 2 the day before yesterday. The next day projection technique is based on a forward shift of the day indexes. That is, today becomes tomorrow, yesterday becomes today and the day before yesterday becomes yesterday. No indexes are used for tomorrow, i.e. $L(0)$ becomes just L, $C(0)$ just C and $O(0)$ just O. The shift results in the following conditions:

$C(0) < L(1)$ and
$L(0) < L$ and
$C   > O$ and
$C   > H(1)$

Notice now that as of the close of a specific day, any of the $C(0)$, $L(0)$, $H(1)$ and $L(1)$ have a specific numeric value. The conditions that involve a quantity with no index are those that must be satisfied by the next day price ranges, and the conditions that involve only indexes are those that must be true as of the close of the last day in order for that pattern to be a candidate for a signal. In the example above, after the shift in indexes, the following condition involves only indexes:

$$C(0) < L(1)$$

and this must be a true condition in order to proceed further. If true, then the following are the conditions that involve no indexes and must be met on the following day:

$$L > L(0) \quad \text{and}$$
$$C > O \quad \text{and}$$
$$C > H(1)$$

The above set of conditions for the values of the low and close of the next day, L and C respectively, must be monitored throughout the trading day to check if any of them becomes false. If, for instance, the low of the next trading day falls below the low of today, $L(0)$, then the pattern cannot generate a trading signal, even if the other conditions are met. The same is true if the market close is either lower than the open or lower than yesterday's high, $H(1)$.

In order to present a more general approach to the next day projection technique, let us consider a price pattern that is formed by n consecutive price bars and has k conditions for generating a trading signal at the close of the nth bar. The k conditions involve only the open, high, low and close of any of the n price bars. The next day projection technique procedure is as follows.

97

Step 1: Label all bars starting from 0, for the last, up to n-1

Step 2: The open, high, low and close for the j bar are denoted as follows, in all k conditions:

$$\text{open} = O(j)$$
$$\text{high} = H(j)$$
$$\text{low} = L(j)$$
$$\text{close} = C(j) \quad , \quad \text{for } j = 0,1,2,\ldots,n\text{-}1$$

Step 3: Derive the new conditions by subtracting 1 from all the indexes found in all k conditions. That is:

$$O(j) \rightarrow O(j\text{-}1)$$
$$H(j) \rightarrow H(j\text{-}1)$$
$$L(j) \rightarrow L(j\text{-}1)$$
$$C(j) \rightarrow C(j\text{-}1), \text{ for all } j = 0,1,2,n\text{-}1$$

Notice that the index "-1" is simply a no-index and is denoted as follows:

$$O(\text{-}1) = O$$
$$H(\text{-}1) = H$$
$$L(\text{-}1) = L$$
$$C(\text{-}1) = C$$

Step 4: After the index shift, there are again k conditions that are separated into two categories:

a) conditions that do not contain O,H,L,C, i.e. do not involve any no-index quantity and

b) conditions that contain any of the O,H,L,C, i.e. involve no-index quantities.

Step 5: Check to see if all of the conditions that do not involve any no-indexes are true. If any untrue then quit. If all true then move to step 6.

Step 6: Solve for the ranges of O,H,L,C that will make all conditions that contain them true.

The last step involves simultaneous solution of a set of conditions. In their simplest form, as in our example, these conditions may be linear inequalities that involve the quantities O,H,L and C. In that case, the solution is simple and so is the code that must be written. More complicated conditions may require some mathematical manipulations to be made. There are many ways to handle this, ranging from manual solutions to the use of symbolic mathematics manipulation packages. When a trading system model is used that is made up of a large number of price patterns then a method to automatically solve the conditions of step 6 is necessary. The procedure to generate the daily entry signals shown in Figure 10-2 of this chapter utilizes a simple symbolic mathematical manipulation algorithm that was especially written for that purpose.

Chapter Eleven

Money Management

Money Management is, all by itself, a very important and often misunderstood subject. Many traders overlook the basics of Money Management that deal with the determination of the amount of capital required to trade a system, which is the most fundamental and useful application of the subject. Instead they make attempts to figure out fancy methods and techniques for varying the number of contracts traded, either in opening or exiting a position. Their intention is to maximize gains. The common mistake is that these methods are rarely treated correctly as an integral part of the model operation logic during the design and simulation phase. One reason for this is the complexity of the code that must be written for the proper implementation of such methods. The result from this oversight is that the expected drawdown is unknown, and there is a danger that the initial trading capital will not be sufficient to cover it.

The discussion that follows gives attention to the quantification of risk as it relates to determining the capital required for trading a mechanical trading system. In that respect, one can distinguish two different types of risk: constant and variable.

Constant risk means assuming the same magnitude of risk whenever initiating a new position. This is the way that most short-term trading systems are used. The risk may be determined by the stop loss per trade and the initial trading capital. For instance, if the stop loss per contract traded is $1,000 and the initial trading capital per contract traded is $50,000, then the risk is 0.02. Thus, it would take 50 losing trades to completely wipe out the initial trading capital, not including commissions paid. Often the maximum risk is stated as a percentage of the trading capital and experts will recommend that it must be less than 0.5%, or 1% or 2%, etc. Another approach involves using the magnitude of the maximum drawdown that will be generated by the trading system during actual operation. However, this number cannot be known in advance but only its simulated estimate, based on historical testing results.

Variable risk per trade implies an adjustment to either the stop loss magnitude or to the number of contracts traded each time per given trading capital, or both. The adjustment can be made according to some algorithmic procedure which is a part of the trading system model, and must be considered as such in the historical testing. For instance, the input to the algorithm can be the market volatility, the rate of real equity increase or decrease, etc. Estimating the risk parameters of such trading systems is not a simple task. There is also no guarantee that these types of systems will produce better results than systems that use a constant number of traded contracts and simple stop loss measures. Experience has shown that increasing the complexity of a trading system, whether in the entry or the exit part, often does not better its performance, and can even result in degradation of the performance.

Determination of Trading Capital

This is probably one of the most important steps in the correct application of trading system models, and therefore cannot be omitted from any discussion of the subject. Underestimation of the capital required to trade a mechanical system may result in losses and eventual failure. That can happen even if the trading system is profitable, due to what is often called "over-trading."

In practice, it is advisable to select a constant risk level and calculate the required minimum trading capital per contract according to the formula:

$$M_s = S / R \qquad\qquad (1)$$

where:

M_s: the trading capital requirement per contract traded, in $.

R: the risk level per trade, in decimals ranging from 0 to 1.

S: the stop loss per trade and per contract traded, in $.

For instance, with a risk level of 0.02, or 2%, and a stop loss of $2,000 per contract traded, the minimum capital requirement is $100,000. If the trader decides to trade one contract per $50,000 of capital, then for the same stop loss value of $2,000 per contract the effective risk is 4%, as can be calculated from equation (1) above.

Equation (1) can apply to trading systems where the stop loss is known in advance and remains at a constant level, such as the short-term trading system based on price patterns discussed in chapter 10. The drawback of this method for estimating the minimum trading capital requirement is that a losing trade does not always generate a dollar loss equal to the stop loss level, since adverse market conditions can result in higher losses. This is especially true when there are "fast" market conditions or illiquid markets, or when the stop order is filled at a market gap opening. However, in the case of short-term trading systems that generate a sufficiently large number of market entry points, or trades, the longer term effect from these adverse market conditions tends to be counterbalanced by favorable conditions that generate higher profits than the selected profit target.

I must make note here that the common practice of most traders is to first select their trading capital size and then calculate the corresponding risk per trade. Then they trade anyway, irrespectively of the level of risk calculated! This is contrary to the method presented above, where the risk level is selected first, and is of much greater importance when a decision must be made whether or not to use a trading system model in actual trading.

Table 11-1 shows a list of examples for the minimum trading capital requirement per contract traded, for various levels of stop loss and risk, assuming one futures contract per trade and no contract accumulation.

The next step in determining the minimum trading capital requirement is to look at the historical performance analysis results for the trading system model under consideration and to note the maximum drawdown.

RISK (%)	STOP LOSS ($)	MIN. CAPITAL ($)
	1,000	100,000
1	2,000	200,000
	5,000	500,000
	1,000	50,000
2	2,000	100,000
	5,000	250,000

Table 11-1: Examples of Trading Capital Requirements

Let

M_d = the trading capital requirement per contract, in $.

D_R = maximum expected drawdown, in $

f = a safety factor multiplier, ex. 1.75, 2, 2.25, 3,..., etc.

MG = the margin requirement per contract, in $

Then

$$M_d = MG + f \times D_R \qquad (2)$$

For example, if the maximum drawdown is $15,000 and the required margin $3,000, then for f set to one the minimum trading capital per contract traded is $18,000. If the safety factor f is set to 2, the new figure is $33,000.

The presence of the safety factor f accounts for a possible future increase in the drawdown amount calculated by the historical testing. Experience has shown that trading systems tend to generate higher drawdowns during actual trading; therefore, a number of at least 2 is recommended for f.

Finally, the determination of M, the minimum trading capital requirement per contract, comes from comparing the results of equations (1) and (2) and selecting the largest figure:

$$M = \max\{M_s, M_d\} \qquad\qquad (3)$$

As an example of the use of equation (3), let us consider a situation with the following parameters:

Risk: R =   0.02 or 2%

Stop: S = $1,000

Drawdown: D_R = $20,000

Margin: MG = $3,000

Safety Factor: f =   3

the above dollar values are per contract traded.

Then, from equation (1):

$$M_s = \$1,000/0.02 = \$50,000$$

and from equation   (2):

$$M_d = \$3,000 + 3 \times \$20,000 = \$63,000$$

Finally, from equation (3):

$$M = \max\{\$50,000,\$63,000\} = \$63,000$$

Now, solving equation (1) for the risk R, we get:

$$R = S/M = \$1,000/\$63,000 = 0.0159 \text{ or } 1.59\%$$

Due to the new capital requirement, the actual risk taken per trade has dropped to 1.59% from 2%, because the initial trading capital per contract was increased from $50,000 to $63,000, using the procedure just outlined.

Of course, the final number is decisively influenced by the selection of the magnitude of the factor f, in equation (2). Increasing the value of f results in increased capital requirements and reduced return on capital, but also reduced risk, in terms of expected equity drawdown and volatility. Decreasing f results in reduced capital requirements and increased return on capital, but higher actual equity drawdown and volatility. There seems to be no procedure to determine f *a priori*, because its optimum value depends on future results that simply cannot be known in advance. The trading system developer and trader must decide based on past experience and future expectations.

Chapter Twelve

Advanced Ways of Using Price Patterns

In order to discuss some advanced ways of using trading systems that are collections of a large number of short-term price patterns, the following definitions are made:

Trading signals that occur one after the other in time are called *successive*. Every signal exits its position with the designated profit target or protective loss before the next signal arrives. The time period between successive occurrences must be short and is usually less than 15 trading periods or bars.

Figure 12-1 shows an example of three successive trading signals. The first signal initiates a position as "ENTRY 1" and exits that position as "EXIT 1." The second trading signal follows after the first has exited and is labeled as "ENTRY 2," with corresponding exit as "EXIT 2." The third signal appears only after the second signal has exited.

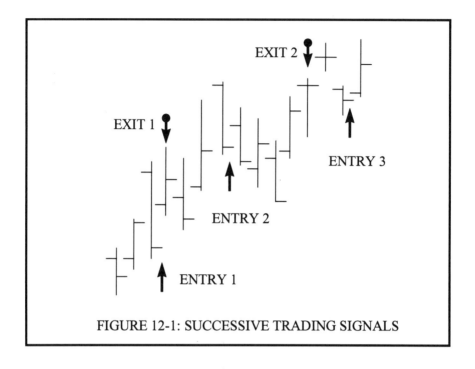

FIGURE 12-1: SUCCESSIVE TRADING SIGNALS

Trading signals that occur while another trading signal has an open position in place are called *coincident*. The trading signal direction must be the same; i.e., a long signal occurs while another long signal is in effect. Occurrence of the second signal must take place at least one bar after the first signal has initiated a position.

Figure 12-2 shows an example of coincident trading signals. The first signal is labeled "ENTRY 1" and is in an open position while the second signal, labeled "ENTRY 2," appears. The third signal, "ENTRY 3," comes after the first signal has exited with "EXIT 1" but while the second signal is still in an open position. Therefore, signals two and three are coincident but signals one and three are successive.

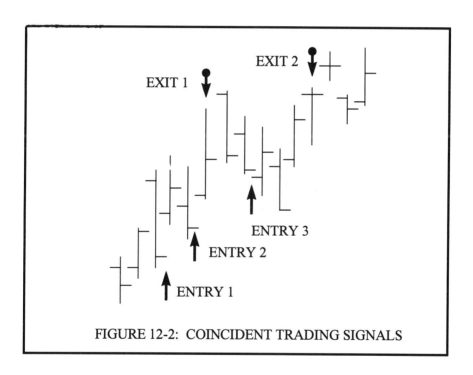

FIGURE 12-2: COINCIDENT TRADING SIGNALS

Trading signals that occur at exactly the same time and all indicate taking a position in the same direction, although signals resulting from different patterns may have different profit targets and stops, are called *clustered.*

Figure 12-3 shows an example of two clustered trading signals, labeled as "ENTRY 1" and "ENTRY 2." Although the two signals exit at different points on the chart, they are clustered because they occur at exactly the same time. Signals one and three are successive because signal three occurs after signal one has exited its position while signals two and three are coincident as signal two is in an open position when signal three arrives.

The examples demonstrate that successive, coincident and clustered trading signals may be formed by any numbers and in any sequence, thus providing many interesting opportunities in trading.

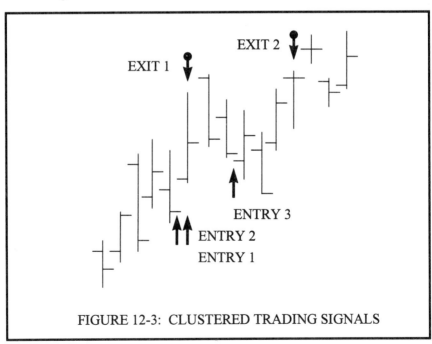

FIGURE 12-3: CLUSTERED TRADING SIGNALS

Trend Following

When short-term patterns generate successive trading signals in the same trading direction, either long or short, it is often possible to achieve partial trend following. However, this is not something that can be achieved by design, but rather a phenomenon that happens occasionally and only by chance. If a trading system model includes a sufficiently large number of short-term patterns, there is a good probability that, during market trends, successive entry signals will allow the trader to capture a good portion of the price trend. In that case, the chances for achieving trend following are increased.

When successive entry signals are generated by the short term trading system model, the net effect is to follow the price direction. However, some short-term patterns often result in losing trades, even if their trading signal direction is in the same direction with the price trend. This happens since short-term patterns tend to ignore the existence of a trend. Nevertheless, a well-designed short-term trading system will cause enough winning trades along the direction of the trend to allow the trader to capture a good portion of it as a net result.

Figures 12-4 and 12-5 show the results of a historical test where successive long position signals are generated when trading T-Bond Futures using a short-term trading system model made up of a collection of patterns, long and short. The period of the test shown is from 3/1/85 to 7/1/85 and the data used is continuously adjusted. Out of the thirteen long trading signals obtained, two are losers and eleven are winners. The total profit of about $9,000 corresponds to a nine full point move per contract in the T-Bonds. Considering then the fact that the magnitude of the trend, as shown in figure 12-4, is roughly thirteen full points, from the bottom formed in March '85 to the peak in June '85, the trading system is capable of capturing 70% of that in profits. In effect then, the trading system, although designed for use in short-term trading, manages to perform as a trend-capturing system in this particular case. When a large collection of patterns is available, capturing a good portion of a price trend is a possibility.

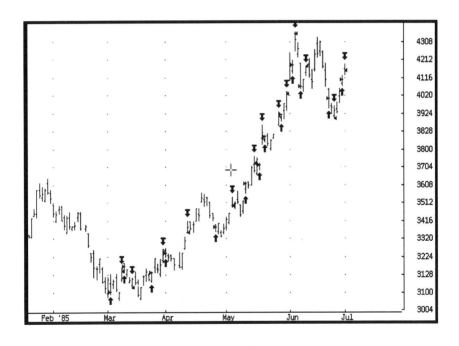

Figure 12-4: Successive Trading Signals on a Trend

Reprinted with permission of Omega Research, Inc.

114

```
HISTORICAL RESULTS : Performance Summary          Model : PATTERN US
Trades  Equity  Chart  Highlights  View-model  Options
Summary, Detailed, Listing
================= US              12/99 - All trades =============
  Test #      1 of    1                    Space bar to toggle display

  Total net profit        $9,130.50
  Gross profit           $11,158.50  Gross loss            $-2,028.00

  Total # of trades            13   Percent profitable          84%
  Number winning trades        11   Number losing trades          2

  Largest winning trade    $1,517.25  Largest losing trade   $-1,014.00
  Average winning trade    $1,014.41  Average losing trade   $-1,014.00
  Ratio avg win/avg loss       1.00  Avg trade (win & loss)    $702.35

  Max consecutive winners       9   Max consecutive losers        1
  Avg # bars in winners         3   Avg # bars in losers          2

  Max closed-out drawdown  $-1,014.00  Max intra-day drawdown  $-1,014.00
  Profit factor                5.50  Max # of contracts held       1
  Account size required    $3,014.00  Return on account          302%

= System Writer Plus ======= Omega Research, Inc. ======= Copyright 1989 =
```

Figure 12-5: Historical Test Results

Reprinted with permission of Omega Research, Inc.

In the case of coincident entry signals, the trader may choose to move the open position profit target and protective stop to new levels. That is, if the trading system has an open long position with a profit target and protective stop already in place, and a newly generated trading signal indicates that a new long position should be taken, then the trader may decide to ignore the new signal, while moving the profit target and protective stop to a new position, as if the new trading signal was being executed. If enough coincident trading signals are generated, the net effect in moving the profit target is to follow a price trend. Moving the protective stop acts in a similar way with trailing stops used in trend-following systems.

If a trading system model allows for variable risk, successive and coincident trading signals may be used to accumulate contracts by adding to existing positions. This must be done only after a careful consideration and estimation of the risk taken in relation to the trading capital.

Modeling and simulating short-term trading system models that are formed by a collection of short-term price patterns, allowing successive and/or coincident trading signals to be used either for adjusting the profit targets and stops, accumulating positions, or both, is a very challenging task.

Estimating the performance characteristics of variable risk trading systems can be difficult due to the complexity of the code that needs to be written. Traders should carefully study those systems and should assume worst-case conditions when estimating the capital requirement. Under-capitalization of a trading account may result in liquidation of positions and in losses, regardless of how profitable the mechanical trading system is.

Pattern Clusters

I have observed that when clusters of trading signals appear, the chance that a profit will be made is better than with a single signal. The trader may treat clusters as a single trading signal and may maintain the same risk level, or may decide to increase the risk level by increasing the number of contracts traded. Again, as with coincident trading signals, this may result in variable risk, so the model performance parameters must be carefully studied during simulation.

A simpler way to use clusters is to consider two different levels of risk, the first being the risk with which the model is designed to operate, called "full" risk, and a second which is a fraction of the first, called "reduced." The trader may decide to use the reduced risk when placing positions resulting from single or isolated trading signals, but may use the full risk when clusters occur. In this way, the worst-case risk is the one used to calculate the minimum trading capital requirements, and when the reduced risk is taken the trading system model operates in a "less risky" mode. However, this trade-off may result in reduced actual profits as compared to trading at full risk, unless enough cluster signals are present.

Summary

When using short-term patterns, a few special cases arise which provide interesting opportunities during trading, such as trend following and contract accumulation.

Alternative ways of using short-term price patterns are many, and their study and analysis can be a very challenging task. In addition to the patterns presented in this chapter, there are many that await exploration as the focus of further research on this subject.

Chapter Thirteen

The p-Indicator

Background

When traders and market analysts refer to indicators, names such as Relative Strength Index (RSI), Directional Movement Index (DMI), and Commodity Channel Index (CCI) immediately come to mind. Although indicators are used in an attempt to forecast future price direction, most have very limited predicting power. The reason for this is the time lag that results from the data-smoothing properties that most of them have built in. In the case of short-term trading, i.e., taking positions in the market that last from one to a few days, most indicators are not effective because they cannot predict short-term market direction. Nevertheless, the concept of looking at a quantity that ranges from 0 to 100, for instance, and generating trading signals based on that, is a very appealing one.

p-Indicator Definition

The p-Indicator is a new concept in defining and constructing an indicator. It is based on the use of short-term price patterns that are created by the market. Since it is a short-term indicator, only the last few days of a particular market are taken into account in the selection of the length of the patterns considered by the indicator. However, *the whole price history* of a particular market is considered when evaluating the past performance of those patterns. The theoretical range of values for the p-Indicator is from 0 to 100, but values between 30 and 70 are normal. The value of the indicator is calculated as a ratio where the numerator is the sum of the percent profitability of the patterns considered in it (each weighted by its corresponding number of occurrences in the data history) and the denominator the sum of all the pattern occurrences. Thus, the p-Indicator can be thought of as having two parts: one to be used for taking long positions and the other for short positions. The calculation of each of the two parts is identical, but in the long part of the indicator the historical percent profitability of the patterns considered is calculated based on taking long positions, and in the short part it is based on taking short positions.

The p-Indicator is then defined as follows:

Let $i = 1,...,N$ to be the number of pattern forms considered,

P_{Li} the percent profitability of each pattern for a long position and P_{Si} for short,

T_i the number of "trades," or occurrences of the

pattern in the price history,

PI_L, the p-Indicator value for long position taking and PI_S, for short. Then

$$PI_L = \frac{\sum\limits_{i=1}^{N} P_{Li} T_i}{\sum\limits_{i=1}^{N} T_i} \qquad PI_S = \frac{\sum\limits_{i=1}^{N} P_{Si} T_i}{\sum\limits_{i=1}^{N} T_i}$$

p-Indicator Properties

Construction:

The p-Indicator is like a weighted probability function. We can think of the historical profitability of a pattern as the probability that the next occurrence of that pattern has in giving a profitable signal. However, the more occurrences that the pattern has, the more "weight" its historical profitability gets in the p-Indicator formula. To illustrate that with an example, let us assume the p-Indicator is made up of only three patterns. For every pattern the corresponding historical profitability, P_{Li}, is calculated for taking a long position. A specific profit target and protective stop are assumed in the calculations. The corresponding number of pattern occurrences is T_i. Let us further assume that the following hypothetical results are obtained:

$P_1 = 60\% \quad T_1 = 150$

$$P_2 = 75\% \quad T_2 = 75$$
$$P_3 = 45\% \quad T_3 = 250$$

The long portion of the p-Indicator is then:

$$PI_L = \frac{60 \times 160 + 75 \times 75 + 45 \times 250}{160 + 75 + 250} = 54.47\,\%$$

Thus, the new weighted profitability is 54.47 %, and that is the value of the p-Indicator for long position taking. Although P_1 and P_2 are 60% and 75% respectively, P_3, which is only 45%, greatly influences the final outcome because it is accompanied by a much higher number of occurrences.

Practical Use:

When the value of PI_L is closer to 100, it indicates a better chance when taking a long position in the corresponding market and when the PI_S value is closer to 100, a better chance for short positions. In practice, numbers from 60 to 70 give good results. Thus, in short-term trading we can use the values of the p-Indicator as follows:

Long Position if $PI_L > a$, $a > 50$

Short Position if $PI_S > b$, $b > 50$

In addition, both long and short parts can be considered together as follows:

Long Position if $PI_L > a$ and $PI_S < b$, $a > 50$

Short Position if $PI_L < b$ and $PI_S > a$, $\qquad$ $b < 50$

Calculation:

Determining the values for the p-Indicator is a calculation-intensive process. This is not very important when considering daily data, but real-time calculations, if desired, can present a problem. Currently, 10 different pattern forms are considered, each for two different sets of targets and stops. For the resulting 20 patterns, the close of the day and the open of the next day is applied as the position entry, thus leaving a total of 40 patterns to be calculated. In the case of daily data, the calculation of the p-Indicator may take from several seconds to a few minutes, depending on processor speed.

Characteristics:

It must be noted that when calculating the past performance of each pattern to be included in the p-Indicator formula, a profit target and a stop loss of specific magnitude are taken into consideration. Thus, *the p-Indicator has the concept of profit target and stop loss incorporated into its definition.* As far as I can tell, this is the only technical indicator with such a property that is found in the literature. Its usefulness results from the fact that conventional indicators generate entry signals for a particular market, long or short, but do not provide any indication whatsoever to the trader as to when to take profits or losses. With the p-Indicator, the profit or loss is known in advance, as soon as the signal is taken. In addition, at any given moment, the p-Indicator *considers the whole price history in its calculations.* This is also the first time, as far as I know, that a trading indicator has been developed with this inherent property.

Example

An example of the performance of the p-Indicator is presented here. The following trading system model is considered:

Long Entry Signal:

If $PI_L > a$ then buy at the open of tomorrow with
  profit target at open of tomorrow + 1 point
  protective stop at open of tomorrow - 1 point

Short Entry Signal:

If $PI_S > b$ then sell at the open of tomorrow with
  profit target at open of tomorrow - 1 point
  protective stop at open of tomorrow + 1 point

Daily data for the day session of the CBOT T-Bond Futures are used from 1/18/90 to 9/21/98. The values of a and b, in the long and short entry signals, are selected to be 60 and 54, respectively. Commission is set to $18 round turn.

The value of the p-Indicator is calculated on a daily basis, with the first day of calculation being the first day of testing, 1/18/90. The historical data for the T-Bond futures contract start at 2/15/83 and are used in the p-Indicator calculations, since the whole price history is required. Figure 13-1 shows the result of the historical test. For this set of values for a and b, the trading system is 67% profitable and has generated 108 trades, which amounts to about one trade per month. The average number of bars for winners is one day and for losers, two days. The maximum intra-day drawdown is $4,586.25 and the return on an account of $7,586.25 is 442%.

Figures 13-2 and 13-3 show the historical test results for long and short trades, respectively. The number of long trades is 52 and that of the short 51, meaning that the trading system operates in both long and short directions with the same trade frequency. The profitability of 69% for the long portion and 66% for the short is quite satisfactory, as are the drawdown and the return on account.

```
HISTORICAL RESULTS : Performance Summary            Model : PINDICATOR
Trades  Equity   Chart   Highlights   View-model   Options
Summary, Detailed, Listing

========== UAN            12/99 - All trades ==========
Test #     1 of    1                      Space bar to toggle display

Total net profit        $33,552.25
Gross profit            $65,146.25  Gross loss              $-31,594.00

Total # of trades            103    Percent profitable            67%
Number winning trades         70    Number losing trades          33

Largest winning trade   $1,450.75  Largest losing trade    $-1,361.75
Average winning trade     $930.66  Average losing trade    $ -957.39
Ratio avg win/avg loss      0.97    Avg trade (win & loss)    $325.75

Max consecutive winners        9    Max consecutive losers         4
Avg # bars in winners          1    Avg # bars in losers           2

Max closed-out drawdown $-4,242.50  Max intra-day drawdown  $-4,586.25
Profit factor               2.06    Max # of contracts held        1
Account size required   $7,586.25  Return on account            442%

== System Writer Plus ====== Omega Research, Inc. ====== Copyright 1989 ==
```

Figure 13-1: p-Indicator Historical Performance

Reprinted with permission of Omega Research, Inc.

```
HISTORICAL RESULTS : Performance Summary              Model : PINDICATOR
Trades   Equity   Chart   Highlights   View-model   Options
Summary, Detailed, Listing
=================== UAN           12/99 - Long trades ================
  Test #      1 of    1                    Space bar to toggle display

Total net profit          $18,251.50
Gross profit              $33,977.00  Gross loss              $-15,725.50

Total # of trades               52   Percent profitable            69%
Number winning trades           36   Number losing trades          16

Largest winning trade      $1,325.75 Largest losing trade     $-1,361.75
Average winning trade        $943.81 Average losing trade      $ -982.84
Ratio avg win/avg loss         0.96  Avg trade (win & loss)     $350.99

Max consecutive winners         7    Max consecutive losers         3
Avg # bars in winners           2    Avg # bars in losers           2

Max closed-out drawdown   $-3,054.00 Max intra-day drawdown   $-3,147.75
Profit factor                  2.16  Max # of contracts held        1
Account size required      $6,147.75 Return on account            296%
== System Writer Plus ======= Omega Research, Inc. ======= Copyright 1989 ==
```

Figure 13-2: p-Indicator Performance - Long Trades

Reprinted with permission of Omega Research, Inc.

```
HISTORICAL RESULTS : Performance Summary              Model : PINDICATOR
Trades    Equity   Chart   Highlights   View-model   Options
Summary, Detailed, Listing
=============== UAN                12/99 - Short trades ==========
 Test #      1 of    1                      Space bar to toggle display

 Total net profit        $15,300.75
 Gross profit            $31,169.25  Gross loss              $-15,868.50

 Total # of trades              51   Percent profitable           66%
 Number winning trades          34   Number losing trades          17

 Largest winning trade   $1,450.75  Largest losing trade    $-1,018.00
 Average winning trade     $916.74  Average losing trade    $ -933.44
 Ratio avg win/avg loss      0.98   Avg trade (win & loss)    $300.01

 Max consecutive winners        7   Max consecutive losers         4
 Avg # bars in winners          1   Avg # bars in losers           3

 Max closed-out drawdown $-3,456.50 Max intra-day drawdown  $-3,456.50
 Profit factor               1.96   Max # of contracts held        1
 Account size required   $6,456.50  Return on account            236%
== System Writer Plus ====== Omega Research, Inc. ====== Copyright 1989 ==
```

Figure 13-3: p-Indicator Performance--Short Trades

Reprinted with permission of Omega Research, Inc.

127

SECTION THREE

PATTERN LIBRARY

Chapter 14

Pattern Library Conventions

In this chapter, I provide guidelines for the use of the library of historical price patterns. These patterns have been found using the automatic pattern search procedure described in chapter 9. Each pattern is defined by the following parameters.

Contract traded:

This is the futures contract for which the pattern applies. Distinction is made for contracts that trade during the day session only and those that include prices from a night session. Traders should exercise caution in applying the proper contract prices if the pattern is employed in actual trading.

Type:

This is the pattern type, as defined in chapter 8. In this pattern library only Exact, Matched, Delay and Inter-Market patterns are shown.

Position:

This is the market position, long or short, that the pattern is to be used for. In the case of Inter-Market patterns, the contract that must be used is also noted, since those patterns are formed in one contract but used to take a position on another.

Profit Target:

The profit target, given in full points, that must be used for trading with the specific pattern. Next to the points, I list the equivalent dollar amount in order to avoid any errors.

Protective Stop:

The stop loss, listed in full points, that must be used in trading. Next to the points, I list the equivalent dollar amount in order to avoid any errors.

Order Entry:

This can be either the close of the day that the pattern formation is completed or the open of the following day.

Order delay:

When a pattern is of the Delay type, the delay in daily bars is listed. That is the number of days that the position entry must be delayed. If, for instance, the delay is 2 and the pattern initiates a position at the open of the next day, then the position must be placed at the open of the day that follows the 2-day delay; that is, at the open of the third day after the pattern formation is completed. If the pattern initiates a position at the close of the day that it is formed and the delay is 3 days then the position must be placed after 3 days.

Logic:

Figure 14-1 shows a pattern that is formed by 5 chart bars. Every bar is labeled above its High, starting from 0 for the last, which is also the bar with which the pattern formation is completed.

For each bar, j, the following notation is used:

$H(j)$ = High of the j bar
$L(j)$ = Low of the j bar
$C(j)$ = Close of the j bar
$O(j)$ = Open of the j bar, $j = 0,1,2,3,\ldots$

The arrows that appear on each bar denote the quantities that appear in the pattern logic. For the graphic example on Figure 14-1, the following quantities are to be included in the logic of the pattern:

Bar 0: $H(0), C(0)$
    1: $C(1)$
    2: $H(2), L(2), C(2)$
    3: $O(3), C(3)$
    4: $O(4), H(4), L(4)$

The logic of the pattern can include only the quantities labeled by the arrows. The remaining quantities are not used, and therefore their corresponding actual position in the pattern formation can be anywhere and is not significant.

133

For each pattern listed in the library, the historical testing results are shown on the opposite page. All historical performance results have been obtained for the time period indicated and assume one contract per trade. All commissions are set to $18 per round turn contract, unless otherwise noted.

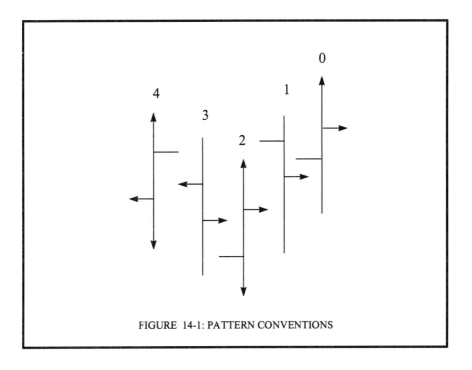

FIGURE 14-1: PATTERN CONVENTIONS

T-BOND PATTERNS

T-BOND PATTERNS
Day Session Only

Pattern Code: UA830406-1
Type: Exact
Position: Long
Profit Target: 1 point = $1,000
Protective Stop: 1 point = $1,000
Order Entry: Close, C(0)
Order delay: 0

Logic: $L(1) > H(2)$ and $H(1) > L(0)$ and $H(3) > L(2)$ and $L(2) > L(3)$ and $L(0) > L(1)$ and $H(0) > H(1)$ and $H(3) > L(2)$

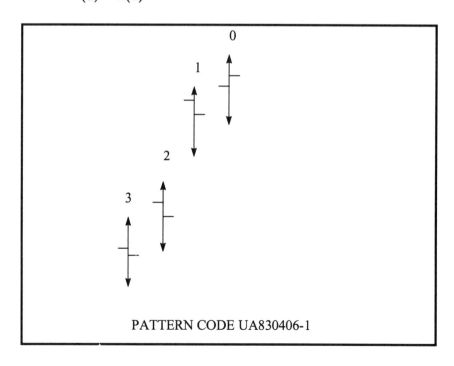

PATTERN CODE UA830406-1

T-BOND PATTERNS
Day Session Only

Pattern Code: UA 830406-1

Historical Performance Results
Period 2/15/83 - 1/7/99

```
HISTORICAL RESULTS : Performance Summary                    Model : UA
Trades  Equity   Chart   Highlights   View-model   Options
Summary, Detailed, Listing

========== UA              12/99 - All trades ==========
Test #      1 of    2                    Space bar to toggle display

Total net profit        $10,660.75
Gross profit            $20,965.75  Gross loss          $-10,305.00

Total # of trades             31    Percent profitable        67%
Number winning trades         21    Number losing trades       10

Largest winning trade    $1,294.50  Largest losing trade  $-1,143.00
Average winning trade      $998.37  Average losing trade  $-1,030.50
Ratio avg win/avg loss       0.97   Avg trade (win & loss)   $343.90

Max consecutive winners        6    Max consecutive losers        2
Avg # bars in winners          4    Avg # bars in losers          2

Max closed-out drawdown  $-2,197.00 Max intra-day drawdown $-2,790.75
Profit factor                2.03   Max # of contracts held       1
Account size required    $5,790.75  Return on account          184%
= System Writer Plus ====== Omega Research, Inc. ====== Copyright 1989 =
```

Reprinted with permission of Omega Research, Inc.

139

T-BOND PATTERNS
Day Session Only

Pattern Code: UA830407-1
Type: Exact
Position: Long
Profit Target: 1 point = $1,000
Protective Stop: 1 point = $1,000
Order Entry: Open of Tomorrow, O
Order delay: 0

Logic: C(0) > C(3) and C(1) > C(2) and C(3) > C(4) and
        C(2)>C(0)

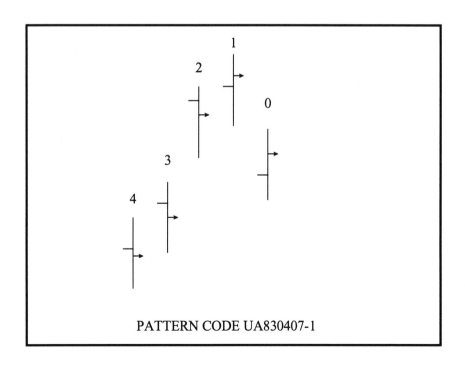

PATTERN CODE UA830407-1

T-BOND PATTERNS
Day Session Only

Pattern Code: UA830407-1

Historical Performance Results
Period 2/15/83 - 1/7/99

```
HISTORICAL RESULTS : Performance Summary                    Model : UA
Trades    Equity    Chart    Highlights    View-model    Options
Summary, Detailed, Listing
─────────────────── UA                12/99 - All trades ═══════════
 Test #      1 of    1                    Space bar to toggle display
 Total net profit          $19,014.75
 Gross profit              $36,664.50  Gross loss          $-17,649.75

 Total # of trades               53    Percent profitable         67%
 Number winning trades           36    Number losing trades        17

 Largest winning trade      $1,482.00  Largest losing trade  $-1,236.75
 Average winning trade      $1,018.46  Average losing trade  $-1,038.22
 Ratio avg win/avg loss          0.98  Avg trade (win & loss)   $358.77

 Max consecutive winners          5    Max consecutive losers        2
 Avg # bars in winners            3    Avg # bars in losers          2

 Max closed-out drawdown    $-2,254.75 Max intra-day drawdown $-2,473.50
 Profit factor                   2.08  Max # of contracts held       1
 Account size required      $5,473.50  Return on account          347%
═ System Writer Plus ═════════ Omega Research, Inc. ═══════ Copyright 1989 ═
```

Reprinted with permission of Omega Research, Inc.

T-BOND PATTERNS
Day Session Only

Pattern Code: UA830826-1
Type: Delay-Exact
Position: Long
Profit Target: 1 point = $1,000
Protective Stop: 1 point = $1,000
Order Entry: Close, C(0)
Order delay: 3

Logic: H(4) > H(5) and H(3) > L(4) and L(5) > H(3) and
        L(4) > L(3) and H(5) > L(5)

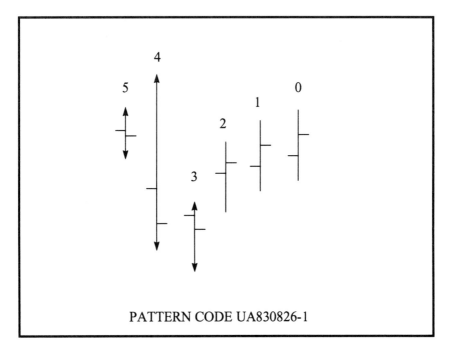

PATTERN CODE UA830826-1

T-BOND PATTERNS
Day Session Only

Pattern Code: UA830826-1

Historical Performance Results
Period 2/15/83 - 1/7/99

```
HISTORICAL RESULTS : Performance Summary                    Model : UA
Trades  Equity  Chart  Highlights  View-model  Options
Summary, Detailed, Listing

================= UA            12/99 - All trades =========
  Test #     1 of    1                     Space bar to toggle display

  Total net profit        $18,389.75
  Gross profit            $35,820.75  Gross loss             $-17,431.00

  Total # of trades              53   Percent profitable          67%
  Number winning trades          36   Number losing trades         17

  Largest winning trade    $1,169.50  Largest losing trade    $-1,143.00
  Average winning trade      $995.02  Average losing trade    $-1,025.35
  Ratio avg win/avg loss        0.97  Avg trade (win & loss)     $346.98

  Max consecutive winners         7   Max consecutive losers        2
  Avg # bars in winners           3   Avg # bars in losers          2

  Max closed-out drawdown  $-3,001.00  Max intra-day drawdown  $-3,001.00
  Profit factor                 2.06  Max # of contracts held       1
  Account size required    $6,001.00  Return on account           306%

== System Writer Plus ======= Omega Research, Inc. ====== Copyright 1989 ==
```

Reprinted with permission of Omega Research, Inc.

T-BOND PATTERNS
Day Session Only

Pattern Code: UA830131-1
Type: Exact
Position: Short
Profit Target: 1 point = $1,000
Protective Stop: 1 point = $1,000
Order Entry: Close, C(0)
Order delay: 0

Logic: C(3) > C(0) and C(1) > C(3) and C(2) > C(1) and
        C(4) > C(2)

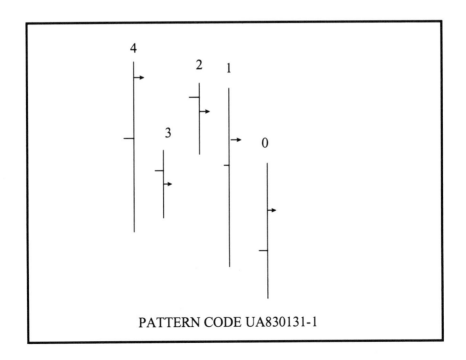

PATTERN CODE UA830131-1

T-BOND PATTERNS
Day Session Only

Pattern Code: UA830131-1

Historical Performance Results

Period 2/15/83 - 1/7/99

```
HISTORICAL RESULTS : Performance Summary                    Model : UA
Trades    Equity   Chart   Highlights   View-model   Options
Summary, Detailed, Listing
════════════ UA                    12/99 - Short trades ════════════
  Test #      1 of    1                      Space bar to toggle display

  Total net profit          $8,929.75
  Gross profit             $16,055.75  Gross loss                $-7,126.00

  Total # of trades               23  Percent profitable              69%
  Number winning trades           16  Number losing trades             7

  Largest winning trade     $1,325.75  Largest losing trade     $-1,018.00
  Average winning trade     $1,003.48  Average losing trade     $-1,018.00
  Ratio avg win/avg loss        0.99  Avg trade (win & loss)      $388.25

  Max consecutive winners         10  Max consecutive losers           2
  Avg # bars in winners            3  Avg # bars in losers             2

  Max closed-out drawdown   $-3,126.00  Max intra-day drawdown   $-3,188.50
  Profit factor                 2.25  Max # of contracts held          1
  Account size required     $6,188.50  Return on account             144%
═ System Writer Plus ═══════ Omega Research, Inc. ═══════ Copyright 1989 ═
```

Reprinted with permission of Omega Research, Inc.

T-BOND PATTERNS
Day Session Only

Pattern Code: UA830304-1
Type: Delay-Exact
Position: Long
Profit Target: 2 points = $2,000
Protective Stop: 2 points = $2,000
Order Entry: Close, C(0)
Order delay: 1

Logic: C(2) > C(4) and C(1) > C(3) and C(4) > C(1)

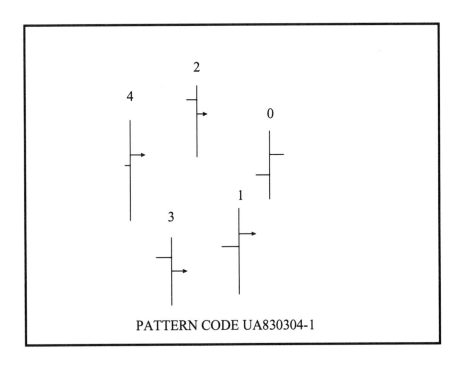

PATTERN CODE UA830304-1

T-BOND PATTERNS
Day Session Only

Pattern Code: UA830304-1

Historical Performance Results

Period 2/15/83 - 1/7/99

```
HISTORICAL RESULTS : Performance Summary              Model : UA
Trades   Equity   Chart   Highlights   View-model   Options
Summary, Detailed, Listing
========================= UA          12/99 - All trades =========
Test #      1 of    1                      Space bar to toggle display

Total net profit        $25,348.25
Gross profit            $43,666.50  Gross loss              $-18,318.25

Total # of trades            31     Percent profitable            70%
Number winning trades        22     Number losing trades           9

Largest winning trade    $2,044.50  Largest losing trade    $-2,111.75
Average winning trade    $1,984.84  Average losing trade    $-2,035.36
Ratio avg win/avg loss       0.98   Avg trade (win & loss)     $817.69

Max consecutive winners       5     Max consecutive losers         2
Avg # bars in winners        13     Avg # bars in losers          13

Max closed-out drawdown  $-4,170.50 Max intra-day drawdown  $-4,170.50
Profit factor                2.38   Max # of contracts held        1
Account size required    $7,170.50  Return on account            353%
= System Writer Plus ====== Omega Research, Inc. ====== Copyright 1989 =
```

Reprinted with permission of Omega Research, Inc.

T-BOND PATTERNS
Day Session Only

Pattern Code: UA830125-1
Type: Exact
Position: Long
Profit Target: 0.5 points = $500
Protective Stop: 0.5 points = $500
Order Entry: Close, C(0)
Order delay: 0

Logic: $H(1) > L(0)$ and $H(0) > L(2)$ and $H(2) > H(0)$ and
       $L(0) > L(1)$ and $L(2) > H(1)$

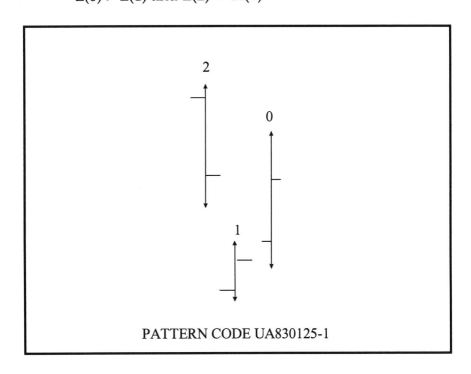

PATTERN CODE UA830125-1

T-BOND PATTERNS
Day Session Only

Pattern Code: UA830125-1

Historical Performance Results
Period 2/15/83 - 1/7/99

```
HISTORICAL RESULTS : Performance Summary                      Model : UA
Trades   Equity   Chart   Highlights   View-model   Options
Summary, Detailed, Listing

═══════════════ UA              12/99 - All trades ═══════════════
 Test #     1 of    1                      Space bar to toggle display

 Total net profit        $8,500.75
 Gross profit           $12,658.00  Gross loss              $-4,157.25

 Total # of trades          26     Percent profitable          73%
 Number winning trades      19     Number losing trades         7

 Largest winning trade   $2,169.50  Largest losing trade    $-1,018.00
 Average winning trade     $666.21  Average losing trade    $ -593.89
 Ratio avg win/avg loss      1.12  Avg trade (win & loss)    $326.95

 Max consecutive winners      6     Max consecutive losers       2
 Avg # bars in winners        1     Avg # bars in losers         1

 Max closed-out drawdown $-1,090.00 Max intra-day drawdown  $-1,090.00
 Profit factor              3.04    Max # of contracts held      1
 Account size required   $4,090.00  Return on account         207%
═ System Writer Plus ════════ Omega Research, Inc. ═══════ Copyright 1989 ═
```

Reprinted with permission of Omega Research, Inc.

T-BOND PATTERNS
Day Session Only

Pattern Code: UA830418-1
Type: Exact
Position: Short
Profit Target: 0.5 points = $500
Protective Stop: 0.5 points = $500
Order Entry: Close, C(0)
Order delay: 0

Logic: H(3) > L(2) and H(2) > L(0) and L(1) > H(3) and
H(0) > H(1) and L(2) > L(3) and L(0) > L(1) and
H(1) > H(2)

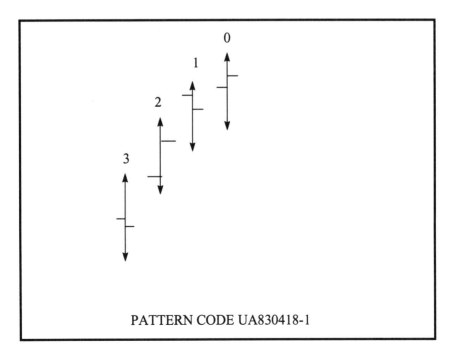

PATTERN CODE UA830418-1

T-BOND PATTERNS
Day Session Only

Pattern Code: UA830418-1

Historical Performance Results
Period 2/15/83 - 1/7/99

```
HISTORICAL RESULTS : Performance Summary                    Model : UA
 Trades   Equity   Chart   Highlights   View-model   Options
Summary, Detailed, Listing
═══════════════════ UA              12/99 - Short trades ═══════════════
  Test #      1 of    1                      Space bar to toggle display

  Total net profit          $6,057.50
  Gross profit             $11,755.50  Gross loss               $-5,698.00

  Total # of trades             35    Percent profitable            68%
  Number winning trades         24    Number losing trades          11

  Largest winning trade     $638.25   Largest losing trade     $ -518.00
  Average winning trade     $489.81   Average losing trade     $ -518.00
  Ratio avg win/avg loss       0.95   Avg trade (win & loss)    $173.07

  Max consecutive winners        4    Max consecutive losers         2
  Avg # bars in winners          1    Avg # bars in losers           1

  Max closed-out drawdown  $-1,072.00 Max intra-day drawdown   $-1,072.00
  Profit factor                2.06   Max # of contracts held        1
  Account size required    $4,072.00  Return on account            148%

══ System Writer Plus ═════════ Omega Research, Inc. ═════════ Copyright 1989 ══
```

Reprinted with permission of Omega Research, Inc.

T-BOND PATTERNS
Including Evening Session

Pattern Code: US800310-1
Type: Exact
Position: Long
Profit Target: 1 point = $1,000
Protective Stop: 1 point = $1,000
Order Entry: Close, C(0)
Order delay: 0

Logic: C(0) > O(2) and O(0) > C(1) and C(2) > O(1) and
        C(1) > C(2) and O(2) > O(0)

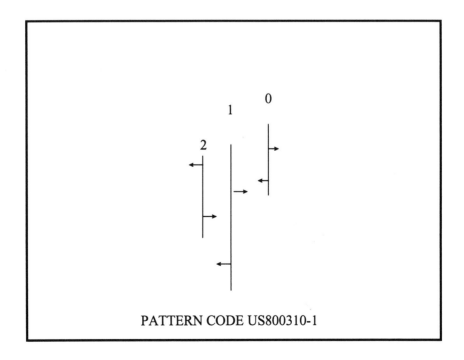

PATTERN CODE US800310-1

T-BOND PATTERNS
Including Evening Session

Pattern Code: US800310-1

Historical Performance Results
Period 1/1/80 - 1/7/99

```
HISTORICAL RESULTS : Performance Summary              Model : US
 Trades  Equity   Chart   Highlights   View-model   Options
Summary, Detailed, Listing
══════════════════ US            12/99 - All trades ═══════════
 Test #      1 of     1                  Space bar to toggle display

 Total net profit       $12,415.50
 Gross profit           $20,653.25  Gross loss             $-8,237.75

 Total # of trades             29   Percent profitable           72%
 Number winning trades         21   Number losing trades          8

 Largest winning trade   $1,013.25  Largest losing trade   $-1,111.75
 Average winning trade     $983.49  Average losing trade   $-1,029.72
 Ratio avg win/avg loss      0.96   Avg trade (win & loss)    $428.12

 Max consecutive winners        5   Max consecutive losers         2
 Avg # bars in winners          4   Avg # bars in losers           2

 Max closed-out drawdown $-2,206.50 Max intra-day drawdown  $-2,447.00
 Profit factor               2.51   Max # of contracts held        1
 Account size required   $5,447.00  Return on account            227%

═ System Writer Plus ════════ Omega Research, Inc. ═══════ Copyright 1989 ═
```

Reprinted with permission of Omega Research, Inc.

T-BOND PATTERNS
Including Evening Session

Pattern Code: US801701-1
Type: Exact
Position: Short
Profit Target: 1 point = $1,000
Protective Stop: 1 point = $1,000
Order Entry: Close, C(0)
Order delay: 0

Logic: C(3) > C(0) and C(2) > C(1) and C(4) > C(2) and
        C(1) > C(3)

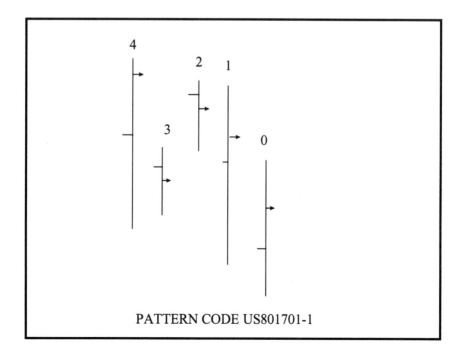

PATTERN CODE US801701-1

T-BOND PATTERNS
Including Evening Session

Pattern Code: US801701-1

Historical Performance Results
Period 1/1/80 - 1/7/99

```
HISTORICAL RESULTS : Performance Summary                    Model : US
Trades   Equity   Chart   Highlights   View-model   Options
Summary, Detailed, Listing
================= US                 12/99 - All trades =======
 Test #       1 of    1                      Space bar to toggle display

 Total net profit        $8,326.50
 Gross profit           $17,676.00  Gross loss              $-9,349.50

 Total # of trades           27     Percent profitable            66%
 Number winning trades       18     Number losing trades           9

 Largest winning trade    $982.00   Largest losing trade    $-1,205.50
 Average winning trade    $982.00   Average losing trade    $-1,038.83
 Ratio avg win/avg loss     0.95    Avg trade (win & loss)    $308.39

 Max consecutive winners     10     Max consecutive losers         2
 Avg # bars in winners        3     Avg # bars in losers           3

 Max closed-out drawdown $-3,126.00 Max intra-day drawdown  $-3,188.50
 Profit factor              1.89    Max # of contracts held        1
 Account size required   $6,188.50  Return on account            134%

-- System Writer Plus ======= Omega Research, Inc. ======= Copyright 1989 ==
```

Reprinted with permission of Omega Research, Inc.

T-BOND PATTERNS
Including Evening Session

Pattern Code: US810220-1
Type: Exact
Position: Short
Profit Target: 1 point = $1,000
Protective Stop: 1 point = $1,000
Order Entry: Open of Tomorrow, O
Order delay: 0

Logic: C(1) > H(2) and C(2) > L(1) and H(0) > C(0) and
        H(2) > L(0) and H(1) > C(1) and L(0) > C(2) and
        C(0) > H(1) and L(1) > L(2)

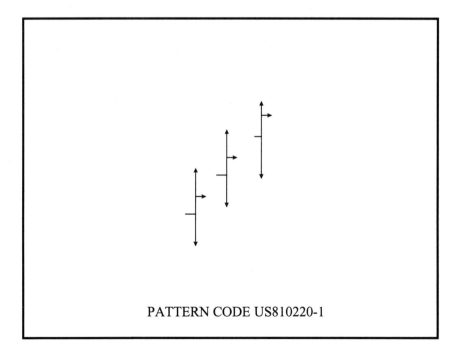

PATTERN CODE US810220-1

T-BOND PATTERNS
Including Evening Session

Pattern Code: US810220-1

Historical Performance Results
Period 1/1/80 - 1/7/99

```
HISTORICAL RESULTS : Performance Summary                    Model : US
 Trades   Equity   Chart   Highlights   View-model   Options
Summary, Detailed, Listing
━━━━━━━━━━━━━━ US                    12/99 - All trades ━━━━━━━
 Test #      1 of    1                    Space bar to toggle display

 Total net profit          $12,586.00
 Gross profit              $17,676.00  Gross loss                $-5,090.00

 Total # of trades                23  Percent profitable               78%
 Number winning trades            18  Number losing trades               5

 Largest winning trade       $982.00  Largest losing trade      $-1,018.00
 Average winning trade       $982.00  Average losing trade      $-1,018.00
 Ratio avg win/avg loss         0.96  Avg trade (win & loss)       $547.22

 Max consecutive winners          8   Max consecutive losers             2
 Avg # bars in winners           1   Avg # bars in losers               2

 Max closed-out drawdown   $-2,036.00  Max intra-day drawdown    $-2,317.25
 Profit factor                  3.47  Max # of contracts held            1
 Account size required      $5,317.25  Return on account               236%

━ System Writer Plus ━━━━━ Omega Research, Inc. ━━━━━ Copyright 1989 ━
```

Reprinted with permission of Omega Research, Inc.

T-BOND PATTERNS
Including Evening Session

Pattern Code: US800111-1
Type: Exact
Position: Short
Profit Target: 2 points = $2,000
Protective Stop: 2 points = $2,000
Order Entry: Close, C(0)
Order delay: 0

Logic: C(2) > C(0) and C(3) > C(2) and C(1) > C(3)

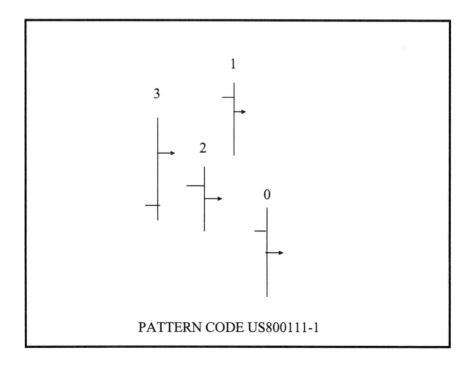

PATTERN CODE US800111-1

T-BOND PATTERNS
Including Evening Session

Pattern Code: US800111-1

Historical Performance Results

Period 1/1/80 - 1/7/99

```
HISTORICAL RESULTS : Performance Summary              Model : US
Trades   Equity   Chart   Highlights   View-model   Options
Summary, Detailed, Listing

═══════════════ US            12/99 - All trades ═══════════
Test #     1 of    1                 Space bar to toggle display

Total net profit      $42,664.25
Gross profit          $90,002.50  Gross loss         $-47,338.25

Total # of trades           69    Percent profitable        65%
Number winning trades       45    Number losing trades       24

Largest winning trade  $2,544.50  Largest losing trade  $-2,580.50
Average winning trade  $2,000.06  Average losing trade  $-1,972.43
Ratio avg win/avg loss      1.01  Avg trade (win & loss)    $618.32

Max consecutive winners      8    Max consecutive losers       2
Avg # bars in winners        9    Avg # bars in losers         9

Max closed-out drawdown $-4,324.00 Max intra-day drawdown $-4,942.25
Profit factor               1.90  Max # of contracts held      1
Account size required  $7,942.25  Return on account         537%
═ System Writer Plus ═══ Omega Research, Inc. ═══ Copyright 1989 ═
```

Reprinted with permission of Omega Research, Inc.

CRUDE OIL PATTERNS

CRUDE OIL PATTERNS

Pattern Code: CL840221-1
Type   Exact
Position: Long
Profit Target: 1 point = $1,000
Protective Stop: 1 point = $1,000
Order Entry: Close, C(0)
Order delay: 0

Logic: L(1) > H(2) and H(1) > L(0) and H(3) > L(2) and
        L(2) > L(3) and L(0) > L(1) and H(0) > H(1) and
        H(3) > L(2)

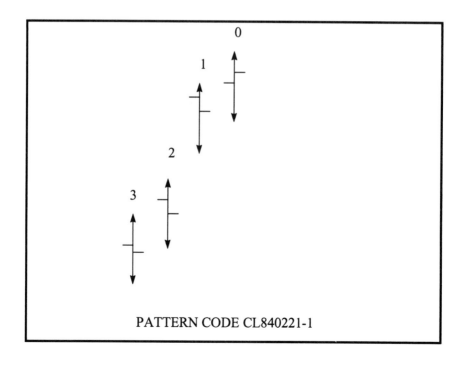

PATTERN CODE CL840221-1

CRUDE OIL PATTERNS

Pattern Code: CL840221-1

Historical Performance Results
Period 2/15/84 - 1/7/99

```
HISTORICAL RESULTS : Performance Summary                    Model : CL
Trades   Equity   Chart   Highlights   View-model   Options
Summary, Detailed, Listing
 ═══════════ CL              12/99 - All trades ═══════
 Test #     1 of    1                    Space bar to toggle display

 Total net prof't        $13,690.00
 Gross profit            $24,958.00  Gross loss           $-11,268.00

 Total # of trades           35      Percent profitable        68%
 Number winning trades       24      Number losing trades      11

 Largest winning trade   $1,512.00   Largest losing trade  $-1,088.00
 Average winning trade   $1,039.92   Average losing trade  $-1,024.36
 Ratio avg win/avg loss      1.02    Avg trade (win & loss)   $391.14

 Max consecutive winners      6      Max consecutive losers      2
 Avg # bars in winners       14      Avg # bars in losers       14

 Max closed-out drawdown $-2,106.00  Max intra-day drawdown $-2,106.00
 Profit factor               2.21    Max # of contracts held     1
 Account size required   $5,106.00   Return on account         268%
 ═ System Writer Plus ════ Omega Research, Inc. ═══ Copyright 1989 ═
```

Reprinted with permission of Omega Research, Inc.

CRUDE OIL PATTERNS

Pattern Code: CL850210-1
Type   Exact
Position: Long
Profit Target: 1 point = $1,000
Protective Stop: 1 point = $1,000
Order Entry: Close, C(0)
Order delay: 0

Logic: C(2) > C(1) and C(0) > C(3) and C(1) > C(4) and
        C(3) > C(2)

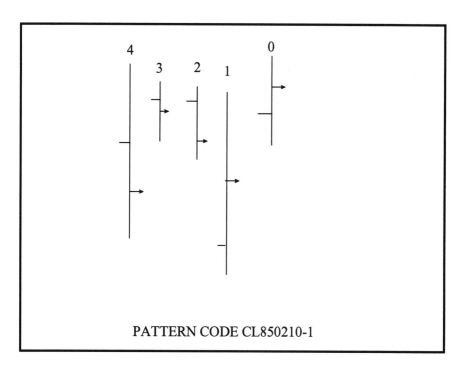

PATTERN CODE CL850210-1

CRUDE OIL PATTERNS

Pattern Code: CL850210-1

Historical Performance Results
Period 2/15/84 - 1/7/99

```
HISTORICAL RESULTS : Performance Summary                    Model : CL
 Trades   Equity   Chart   Highlights   View-model   Options
Summary, Detailed, Listing

=================== CL ===========  12/99 - All trades ================
 Test #      1 of     1                    Space bar to toggle display

 Total net profit          $9,528.00
 Gross profit             $17,224.00  Gross loss               $-7,696.00

 Total # of trades               24  Percent profitable              70%
 Number winning trades           17  Number losing trades              7

 Largest winning trade     $1,402.00  Largest losing trade     $-1,588.00
 Average winning trade     $1,013.18  Average losing trade     $-1,099.43
 Ratio avg win/avg loss        0.92  Avg trade (win & loss)      $397.00

 Max consecutive winners         6  Max consecutive losers            2
 Avg # bars in winners          11  Avg # bars in losers              7

 Max closed-out drawdown  $-2,072.00  Max intra-day drawdown   $-2,072.00
 Profit factor                 2.24  Max # of contracts held           1
 Account size required     $5,072.00  Return on account              187%

== System Writer Plus ====== Omega Research, Inc. ====== Copyright 1989 ==
```

Reprinted with permission of Omega Research, Inc.

CRUDE OIL PATTERNS

Pattern Code: CL850919-1
Type   Exact
Position: Long
Profit Target: 1 point = $1,000
Protective Stop: 1 point = $1,000
Order Entry: Close, C(0)
Order delay: 0

Logic: H(1) > H(2) and L(0) > L(1) and H(0) > C(0) and
        H(2) > O(0) and O(0) > L(0) and L(0) > L(1) and
        L(1) > L(2)

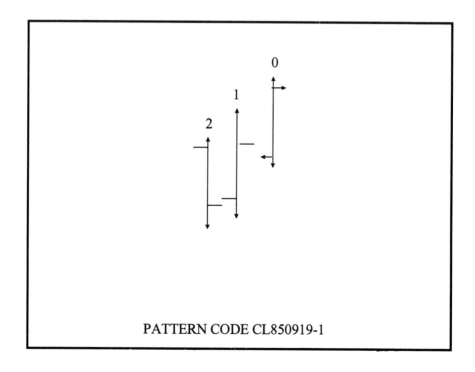

PATTERN CODE CL850919-1

CRUDE OIL PATTERNS

Pattern Code: CL850919-1

Historical Performance Results
Period 2/15/84 - 1/7/99

```
HISTORICAL RESULTS : Performance Summary                    Model : CL
Trades   Equity   Chart   Highlights   View-model   Options
Summary, Detailed, Listing

============= CL                    12/99 - All trades =============
Test #        1 of    1                    Space bar to toggle display

Total net profit          $13,416.00
Gross profit              $26,362.00   Gross loss             $-12,946.00

Total # of trades                 38   Percent profitable             68%
Number winning trades             26   Number losing trades            12

Largest winning trade      $1,332.00   Largest losing trade     $-1,628.00
Average winning trade      $1,013.92   Average losing trade     $-1,078.83
Ratio avg win/avg loss          0.94   Avg trade (win & loss)      $353.05

Max consecutive winners            6   Max consecutive losers           2
Avg # bars in winners              8   Avg # bars in losers            12

Max closed-out drawdown   $-2,036.00   Max intra-day drawdown   $-2,668.00
Profit factor                   2.04   Max # of contracts held          1
Account size required      $5,668.00   Return on account             236%

= System Writer Plus ======= Omega Research, Inc. ====== Copyright 1989 =
```

Reprinted with permission of Omega Research, Inc.

CRUDE OIL PATTERNS

Pattern Code: CL841206-1
Type   Exact
Position: Long
Profit Target: 1 point = $1,000
Protective Stop: 1 point = $1,000
Order Entry: Open of Tomorrow, O
Order delay: 0

Logic: H(2) > C(2) and L(0) > H(2) and H(0) > H(1) and
        C(0) > L(0) and H(1) > C(1) and C(2) > L(1) and
        L(1) > L(2) and C(1) > C(0)

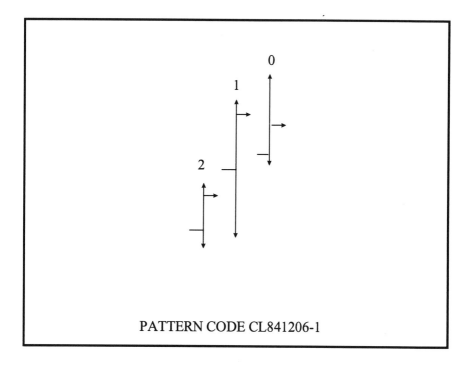

PATTERN CODE CL841206-1

CRUDE OIL PATTERNS

Pattern Code: CL841206-1

Historical Performance Results
Period 2/15/84 - 1/7/99

```
HISTORICAL RESULTS : Performance Summary                    Model : CL
Trades   Equity   Chart   Highlights   View-model   Options
Summary, Detailed, Listing

========================== CL            12/99 - All trades ============
 Test #      1 of    1                        Space bar to toggle display

 Total net profit          $10,004.00
 Gross profit              $21,202.00  Gross loss              $-11,198.00

 Total # of trades                 32  Percent profitable              65%
 Number winning trades             21  Number losing trades            11

 Largest winning trade      $1,182.00  Largest losing trade     $-1,018.00
 Average winning trade      $1,009.62  Average losing trade     $-1,018.00
 Ratio avg win/avg loss          0.99  Avg trade (win & loss)      $312.62

 Max consecutive winners           7   Max consecutive losers           3
 Avg # bars in winners            12   Avg # bars in losers             8

 Max closed-out drawdown    $-3,090.00  Max intra-day drawdown   $-3,310.00
 Profit factor                   1.89  Max # of contracts held          1
 Account size required      $6,310.00  Return on account              158%

== System Writer Plus ======== Omega Research, Inc. ======= Copyright 1989 ==
```

Reprinted with permission of Omega Research, Inc.

SWISS FRANC PATTERNS

SWISS FRANC PATTERNS

Pattern Code: SF830520-1
Type   Exact
Position: Short
Profit Target: 1 point = $1,250
Protective Stop: 1 point = $1,250
Order Entry: Close, C(0)
Order delay: 0

Logic: C(1) > C(0) and C(2) > O(1) and O(0) > C(1) and
        O(2) > C(2) and O(1) > O(0)

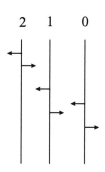

PATTERN CODE SF830520-1

SWISS FRANC PATTERNS

Pattern Code: SF830520-1

Historical Performance Results
Period 2/15/83 - 1/7/99

```
HISTORICAL RESULTS : Performance Summary                    Model : SF
Trades   Equity   Chart   Highlights   View-model   Options
Summary, Detailed, Listing
┌──────────────────── SF            12/99 - All trades ────────────────┐
│ Test #      1 of    1                      ` Space bar to toggle display│
│                                                                          │
│ Total net profit        $13,796.00                                       │
│ Gross profit            $25,220.50  Gross loss            $-11,424.50     │
│                                                                          │
│ Total # of trades              28   Percent profitable          67%      │
│ Number winning trades          19   Number losing trades          9      │
│                                                                          │
│ Largest winning trade    $2,057.00  Largest losing trade     $-1,280.50  │
│ Average winning trade    $1,327.39  Average losing trade      $-1,269.39  │
│ Ratio avg win/avg loss        1.05  Avg trade (win & loss)       $492.71  │
│                                                                          │
│ Max consecutive winners         9   Max consecutive losers          3    │
│ Avg # bars in winners           5   Avg # bars in losers          11     │
│                                                                          │
│ Max closed-out drawdown  $-3,840.00 Max intra-day drawdown    $-4,341.50 │
│ Profit factor                  2.21 Max # of contracts held         1    │
│ Account size required    $7,341.50  Return on account            187%    │
└═ System Writer Plus ════════ Omega Research, Inc. ═══════ Copyright 1989 ═┘
```

Reprinted with permission of Omega Research, Inc.

SWISS FRANC PATTERNS

Pattern Code: SF831011-3
Type   Matched
Position: Short
Profit Target: 1 point = $1,250
Protective Stop: 1 point = $1,250
Order Entry: Open of Tomorrow, O
Order delay: 0

Logic: C(3) > C(2) and C(2) > C(1) and C(4) > C(0) and
        ((C(0) > C(3)) or (C(0) > C(2) and C(3) > C(4)))

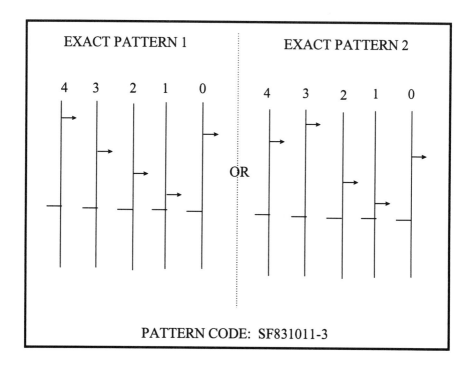

EXACT PATTERN 1   EXACT PATTERN 2

OR

PATTERN CODE: SF831011-3

SWISS FRANC PATTERNS

Pattern Code: SF831011-3

Historical Performance Results
Period 2/15/83 - 1/7/99

```
HISTORICAL RESULTS : Performance Summary                    Model : SF
 Trades   Equity   Chart   Highlights   View-model   Options
Summary, Detailed, Listing
━━━━━━━━━━━━━━━━━━━ SF              12/99 - All trades ━━━━━━━━━
 Test #      1 of    1                    Space bar to toggle display

 Total net profit         $17,467.50
 Gross profit             $35,051.50  Gross loss              $-17,584.00

 Total # of trades            40      Percent profitable           67%
 Number winning trades        27      Number losing trades          13

 Largest winning trade    $1,782.00   Largest losing trade    $-1,730.50
 Average winning trade    $1,298.20   Average losing trade    $-1,352.62
 Ratio avg win/avg loss       0.96    Avg trade (win & loss)     $436.69

 Max consecutive winners       5      Max consecutive losers         1
 Avg # bars in winners         5      Avg # bars in losers           6

 Max closed-out drawdown  $-1,730.50  Max intra-day drawdown  $-2,305.50
 Profit factor                1.99    Max # of contracts held        1
 Account size required    $5,305.50   Return on account           329%
━━━ System Writer Plus ━━━━━━ Omega Research, Inc. ━━━━━━ Copyright 1989 ━━
```

Reprinted with permission of Omega Research, Inc.

175

SWISS FRANC PATTERNS

Pattern Code: SF830519-1
Type   Delay-Exact
Position: Long
Profit Target: 1 point = $1,250
Protective Stop: 1 point = $1,250
Order Entry: Close, C(0)
Order delay: 3

Logic: C(7) > C(3) and C(6) > C(5) and C(4) > C(7) and
       C(5) > C(4)

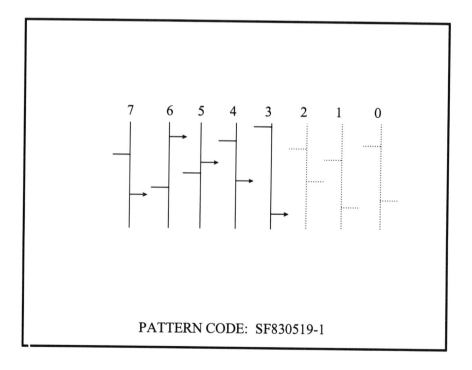

PATTERN CODE: SF830519-1

SWISS FRANC PATTERNS

Pattern Code: SF830519-1

Historical Performance Results
Period 2/15/83 - 1/7/99

```
HISTORICAL RESULTS : Performance Summary              Model : SF
Trades   Equity   Chart   Highlights   View-model   Options
Summary, Detailed, Listing

═══════════ SF              12/99 - All trades ═══════════
Test #     1 of   1                   Space bar to toggle display

Total net profit        $20,011.50
Gross profit            $30,480.50  Gross loss          $-10,469.00

Total # of trades           32      Percent profitable        75%
Number winning trades       24      Number losing trades        8

Largest winning trade    $1,819.50  Largest losing trade  $-1,468.00
Average winning trade    $1,270.02  Average losing trade  $-1,308.62
Ratio avg win/avg loss       0.97   Avg trade (win & loss)   $625.36

Max consecutive winners     11      Max consecutive losers       2
Avg # bars in winners        4      Avg # bars in losers         3

Max closed-out drawdown  $-2,736.00 Max intra-day drawdown $-2,798.50
Profit factor                2.91   Max # of contracts held      1
Account size required    $5,798.50  Return on account         345%

═ System Writer Plus ════ Omega Research, Inc. ════ Copyright 1989 ═
```

Reprinted with permission of Omega Research, Inc.

S&P 500 PATTERNS

S&P 500 PATTERNS

Pattern Code: SP830825-1
Type   Exact
Position: Long
Profit Target: 10 points = $2,500
Protective Stop: 10 points = $2,500
Order Entry: Open of Tomorrow, O
Order delay: 0

Logic: H(0) > L(1) and L(2) > H(0) and H(1) > L(2) and
        H(2) > L(3) and L(1) > L(0) and L(3) > H(1) and
        H(3) > H(2)

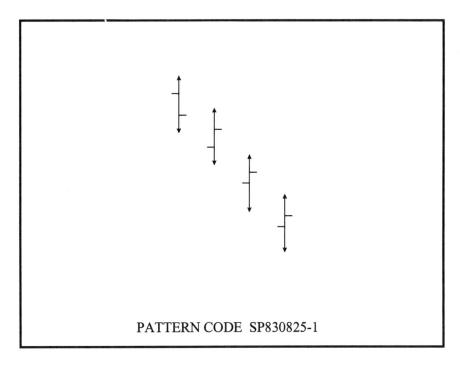

PATTERN CODE SP830825-1

S&P 500 PATTERNS

Pattern Code: SP830825-1

Historical Performance Results
Period 2/15/83 - 1/7/99

```
HISTORICAL RESULTS : Performance Summary                    Model : SP
 Trades   Equity   Chart   Highlights   View-model   Options
Summary, Detailed, Listing
=============== SP                 12/99 - All trades ==============
 Test #     1 of    1                   Space bar to toggle display

 Total net profit        $27,576.50
 Gross profit            $47,720.50  Gross loss              $-20,144.00

 Total # of trades             27   Percent profitable            70%
 Number winning trades         19   Number losing trades           8

 Largest winning trade    $2,982.00 Largest losing trade    $-2,518.00
 Average winning trade    $2,511.61 Average losing trade    $-2,518.00
 Ratio avg win/avg loss        1.00 Avg trade (win & loss)   $1,021.35

 Max consecutive winners        6   Max consecutive losers         3
 Avg # bars in winners          22  Avg # bars in losers           6

 Max closed-out drawdown  $-7,554.00 Max intra-day drawdown  $-7,941.50
 Profit factor                 2.37 Max # of contracts held        1
 Account size required    $24,941.50 Return on account            110%

= System Writer Plus ======= Omega Research, Inc. ======= Copyright 1989 =
```

Reprinted with permission of Omega Research, Inc.

S&P 500 PATTERNS

Pattern Code: SP830120-1
Type   Exact
Position: Long
Profit Target: 10 points = $2,500
Protective Stop: 10 points = $2,500
Order Entry: Open of Tomorrow, O
Order delay: 0

Logic: H(0) > C(0) and L(2) > L(0) and H(1) > H(0) and
        H(2) > H(1) and L(0) > L(1) and C(0) > L(2)

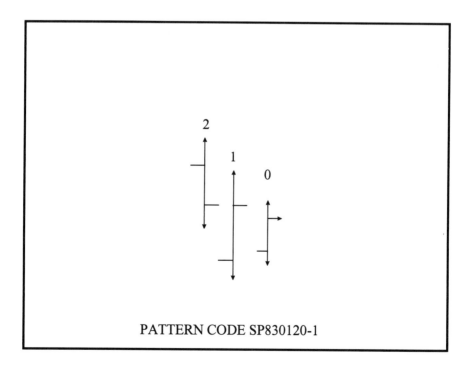

PATTERN CODE SP830120-1

S&P 500 PATTERNS

Pattern Code: SP830120-1

Historical Performance Results
Period 2/15/83 - 1/7/99

```
HISTORICAL RESULTS : Performance Summary                    Model : SP
Trades   Equity   Chart   Highlights   View-model   Options
Summary, Detailed, Listing
=============== SP ==============      12/99 - All trades ===============
 Test #      1 of    1                         Space bar to toggle display

 Total net profit         $34,387.50
 Gross profit             $79,711.50  Gross loss              $-45,324.00

 Total # of trades              50    Percent profitable             64%
 Number winning trades          32    Number losing trades           18

 Largest winning trade     $2,707.00  Largest losing trade    $-2,518.00
 Average winning trade     $2,490.98  Average losing trade    $-2,518.00
 Ratio avg win/avg loss         0.99  Avg trade (win & loss)     $687.75

 Max consecutive winners         5    Max consecutive losers          3
 Avg # bars in winners          16    Avg # bars in losers           10

 Max closed-out drawdown   $-7,590.00 Max intra-day drawdown  $-8,315.00
 Profit factor                  1.76  Max # of contracts held         1
 Account size required     $25,315.00 Return on account             135%
== System Writer Plus ======= Omega Research, Inc. ===== Copyright 1989 ==
```

Reprinted with permission of Omega Research, Inc.

S&P 500 PATTERNS

Pattern Code: SP830330-1
Type   Exact
Position: Long
Profit Target: 10 points = $2,500
Protective Stop: 10 points = $2,500
Order Entry: Open of Tomorrow, O
Order delay: 0

Logic: H(0) > C(0) and L(2) > L(1) and H(1) > H(2) and
        H(2) > L(0) and C(0) > H(1) and L(0) > L(2)

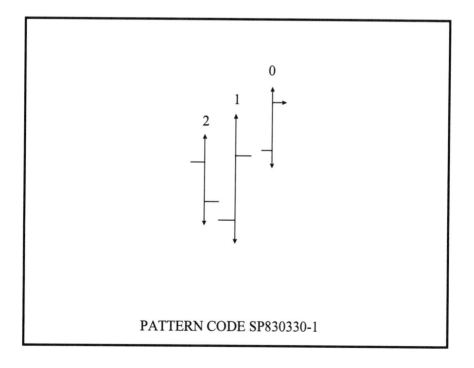

PATTERN CODE SP830330-1

S&P 500 PATTERNS

Pattern Code: SP830330-1

Historical Performance Results
Period 2/15/83 - 1/7/99

```
HISTORICAL RESULTS : Performance Summary                       Model : SP
Trades    Equity    Chart    Highlights    View-model    Options
Summary, Detailed, Listing

=================== SP            12/99 - All trades ================
  Test #      1 of    1                      Space bar to toggle display

  Total net profit        $36,684.00
  Gross profit            $64,807.00  Gross loss              $-28,123.00

  Total # of trades           37     Percent profitable             70%
  Number winning trades       26     Number losing trades           11

  Largest winning trade    $2,719.50  Largest losing trade     $-2,818.00
  Average winning trade    $2,492.58  Average losing trade     $-2,556.64
  Ratio avg win/avg loss       0.97  Avg trade (win & loss)      $991.46

  Max consecutive winners      7     Max consecutive losers          2
  Avg # bars in winners       11     Avg # bars in losers           15

  Max closed-out drawdown  $-5,036.00  Max intra-day drawdown   $-5,198.50
  Profit factor                2.30  Max # of contracts held         1
  Account size required   $22,198.50  Return on account             165%

== System Writer Plus ======== Omega Research, Inc. ======= Copyright 1989 ==
```

Reprinted with permission of Omega Research, Inc.

185

SILVER PATTERNS

SILVER PATTERNS

Pattern Code: SI830520-1
Type   Exact
Position: Short
Profit Target: 40 points = $2,000
Protective Stop: 40 points = $2,000
Order Entry: Open of Tomorrow, O
Order delay: 0

Logic: H(0) > C(1) and L(2) > H(0) and H(1) > C(2) and
        C(2) > L(2) and L(1) > C(0) and C(0) > L(0) and
        H(2) > H(1) and C(1) > L(1)

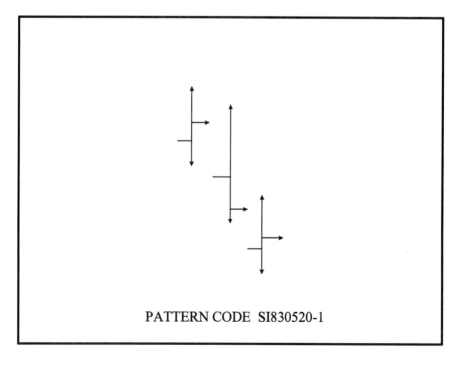

PATTERN CODE SI830520-1

SILVER PATTERNS

Pattern Code: SI830520-1

Historical Performance Results
Period 2/15/83 - 1/7/99

```
HISTORICAL RESULTS : Performance Summary                    Model : SI
Trades    Equity   Chart    Highlights    View-model    Options
Summary, Detailed, Listing

========== SI              12/99 - Short trades ==========
  Test #      1 of     1                    Space bar to toggle display

  Total net profit        $20,248.00
  Gross profit            $34,374.00  Gross loss            $-14,126.00

  Total # of trades            24     Percent profitable         70%
  Number winning trades        17     Number losing trades         7

  Largest winning trade    $2,457.00  Largest losing trade    $-2,018.00
  Average winning trade    $2,022.00  Average losing trade    $-2,018.00
  Ratio avg win/avg loss       1.00   Avg trade (win & loss)     $843.67

  Max consecutive winners       5     Max consecutive losers        2
  Avg # bars in winners         44    Avg # bars in losers         25

  Max closed-out drawdown $-4,072.00  Max intra-day drawdown  $-5,061.00
  Profit factor                2.43   Max # of contracts held       1
  Account size required    $8,061.00  Return on account          251%
=== System Writer Plus ====== Omega Research, Inc. ====== Copyright 1989 ==
```

Reprinted with permission of Omega Research, Inc.

SILVER PATTERNS

Pattern Code: SI830630-1
Type   Delay-Exact
Position: Short
Profit Target: 20 points = $1,000
Protective Stop: 20 points = $1,000
Order Entry: Open of Tomorrow, O
Order delay: 3

Logic: C(4) > C(3) and C(6) > C(4) and C(7) > C(6) and
        C(3) > C(5)

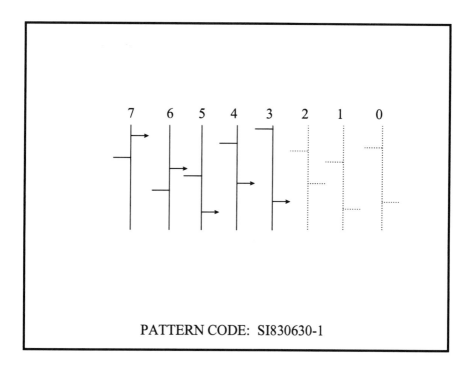

PATTERN CODE: SI830630-1

SILVER PATTERNS

Pattern Code: SI830630-1

Historical Performance Results
Period 2/15/83 - 1/7/99

```
HISTORICAL RESULTS : Performance Summary                    Model : SI
Trades   Equity   Chart   Highlights   View-model   Options
Summary, Detailed, Listing
================ SI            12/99 - All trades ================
Test #      1 of    1                  Space bar to toggle display

Total net profit          $9,930.00
Gross profit             $22,771.00  Gross loss               $-12,841.00

Total # of trades              35    Percent profitable            65%
Number winning trades          23    Number losing trades           12

Largest winning trade     $1,067.00  Largest losing trade      $-1,543.00
Average winning trade       $990.04  Average losing trade      $-1,070.08
Ratio avg win/avg loss        0.93   Avg trade (win & loss)      $283.71

Max consecutive winners         5    Max consecutive losers          2
Avg # bars in winners          12    Avg # bars in losers            3

Max closed-out drawdown  $-2,633.00  Max intra-day drawdown    $-3,097.00
Profit factor                 1.77   Max # of contracts held         1
Account size required     $6,097.00  Return on account             162%

== System Writer Plus ====== Omega Research, Inc. ====== Copyright 1989 ==
```

Reprinted with permission of Omega Research, Inc.

INTER-MARKET PATTERNS

S&P 500 PATTERNS
LONG T-BONDS, DAY SESSION

Pattern Code: SP830128-2
Type   Exact
Position: Long T-BONDS
Profit Target: 1 point = $1,000
Protective Stop: 1 point = $1,000
Order Entry: Open of Tomorrow, O
Order delay: 0

Logic: H(2) > C(2) and L(0) > L(1) and H(0) > H(1) and
        C(0) > L(1) and H(1) > C(1) and C(2) > L(2) and
        L(1) > H(2) and C(1) > C(0)

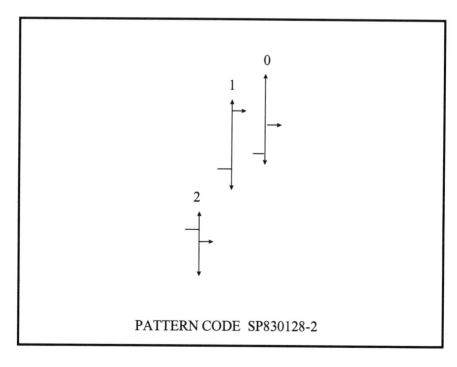

PATTERN CODE SP830128-2

S&P 500 PATTERNS
LONG T-BONDS, DAY SESSION

Pattern Code: SP830128-2

Historical Performance Results
Period 2/15/83 - 1/7/99

```
HISTORICAL RESULTS : Performance Summary                    Model : SP TO US
Trades   Equity   Chart   Highlights   View-model   Options
Summary, Detailed, Listing

━━━━━━━━━━━━━━ UA                    12/99 - All trades ━━━━━━━━━
Test #      1 of    1                      Space bar to toggle display

Total net profit          $11,885.25
Gross profit              $16,975.25  Gross loss                 $-5,090.00

Total # of trades                 22  Percent profitable                77%
Number winning trades             17  Number losing trades               5

Largest winning trade      $1,232.00  Largest losing trade       $-1,018.00
Average winning trade        $998.54  Average losing trade       $-1,018.00
Ratio avg win/avg loss          0.98  Avg trade (win & loss)        $540.24

Max consecutive winners           11  Max consecutive losers             3
Avg # bars in winners              1  Avg # bars in losers               3

Max closed-out drawdown    $-3,054.00  Max intra-day drawdown     $-3,085.25
Profit factor                   3.34  Max # of contracts held            1
Account size required      $6,085.25  Return on account               195%

━ System Writer Plus ━━━━━━ Omega Research, Inc. ━━━━━━ Copyright 1989 ━
```

Reprinted with permission of Omega Research, Inc.

S&P 500 PATTERNS
LONG T-BONDS, DAY SESSION

Pattern Code: SP830107-2
Type   Exact
Position: Long T-BONDS
Profit Target: 1 point = $1,000
Protective Stop: 1 point = $1,000
Order Entry: Open of Tomorrow, O
Order delay: 0

Logic: $H(2) > C(2)$ and $L(0) > H(2)$ and $H(0) > H(1)$ and
        $C(0) > C(1)$ and $H(1) > C(0)$ and $C(2) > L(1)$ and
        $L(1) > L(2)$ and $C(1) > L(0)$

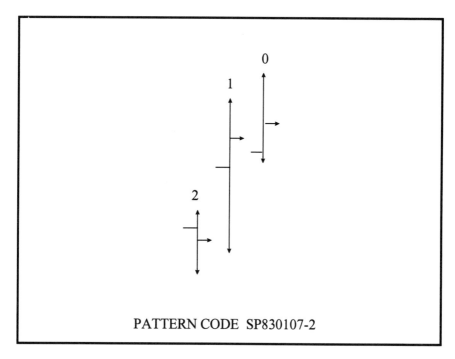

PATTERN CODE SP830107-2

S&P 500 PATTERNS
LONG T-BONDS, DAY SESSION

Pattern Code: SP830107-2

Historical Performance Results
Period 2/15/83 - 1/7/99

```
HISTORICAL RESULTS : Performance Summary                Model : SP TO US
Trades  Equity  Chart  Highlights  View-model  Options
Summary, Detailed, Listing

══════════════ UA              12/99 - All trades ══════════════
Test #      1 of    1                      Space bar to toggle display

Total net profit          $8,768.75
Gross profit             $17,631.50  Gross loss                $-8,862.75

Total # of trades              25    Percent profitable              68%
Number winning trades          17    Number losing trades             8

Largest winning trade     $1,825.75  Largest losing trade      $-1,611.75
Average winning trade     $1,037.15  Average losing trade      $-1,107.84
Ratio avg win/avg loss         0.94  Avg trade (win & loss)       $350.75

Max consecutive winners         6    Max consecutive losers           2
Avg # bars in winners           2    Avg # bars in losers             3

Max closed-out drawdown   $-2,629.75 Max intra-day drawdown    $-2,973.50
Profit factor                  1.99  Max # of contracts held          1
Account size required     $5,973.50  Return on account             146%

═ System Writer Plus ═══════ Omega Research, Inc. ═══════ Copyright 1989 ═
```

Reprinted with permission of Omega Research, Inc.

S&P 500 PATTERNS
LONG T-BONDS

Pattern Code: SP830825-2
Type   Exact
Position: Long T-BONDS
Profit Target: 2 points = $2,000
Protective Stop: 2 points = $2,000
Order Entry: Open of Tomorrow, O
Order delay: 0

Logic: H(2) > L(3) and L(2) > H(0) and H(1) > L(2) and
H(0) > L(1) and L(3) > H(1) and H(3) > H(2) and
L(1) > L(0)

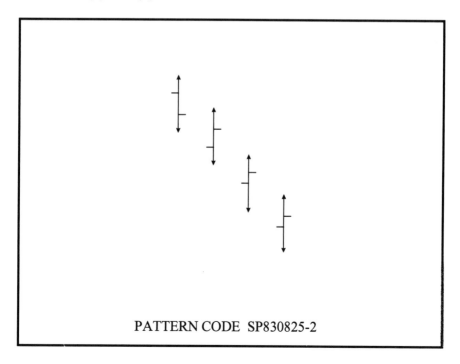

PATTERN CODE SP830825-2

S&P 500 PATTERNS
LONG T-BONDS

Pattern Code: SP830825-2

Historical Performance Results
Period 2/15/83 - 1/7/99

```
HISTORICAL RESULTS : Performance Summary                    Model : SP TO US
Trades   Equity   Chart   Highlights   View-model   Options
Summary, Detailed, Listing
========================= US              12/99 - All trades ============
Test #        1 of    1                      Space bar to toggle display

Total net profit          $17,942.00
Gross profit              $40,171.25  Gross loss              $-22,229.25

Total # of trades              31     Percent profitable           64%
Number winning trades          20     Number losing trades          11

Largest winning trade     $2,263.25   Largest losing trade     $-2,049.25
Average winning trade     $2,008.56   Average losing trade     $-2,020.84
Ratio avg win/avg loss         0.99   Avg trade (win & loss)      $578.77

Max consecutive winners         7     Max consecutive losers         2
Avg # bars in winners          14     Avg # bars in losers           6

Max closed-out drawdown   $-4,036.00  Max intra-day drawdown   $-5,317.25
Profit factor                  1.81   Max # of contracts held        1
Account size required     $8,317.25   Return on account            215%
= System Writer Plus ========= Omega Research, Inc. ======= Copyright 1989 =
```

Reprinted with permission of Omega Research, Inc.

S&P 500 PATTERNS
LONG T-BONDS, DAY SESSION

Pattern Code: SP830405-2
Type   Exact
Position: Long T-BONDS
Profit Target: 1 point = $1,000
Protective Stop: 1 point = $1,000
Order Entry: Open of Tomorrow, O
Order delay: 0

Logic: H(1) > L(1) and L(2) > L(0) and H(0) > H(1) and
        H(2) > H(0) and L(1) > L(0)

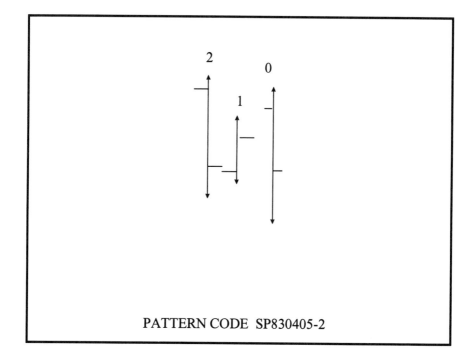

PATTERN CODE SP830405-2

S&P 500 PATTERNS
LONG T-BONDS, DAY SESSION

Pattern Code: SP830405-2

Historical Performance Results
Period 2/15/83 - 1/7/99

```
HISTORICAL RESULTS : Performance Summary              Model : SP TO US
Trades   Equity   Chart   Highlights   View-model   Options
Summary, Detailed, Listing

================= UA                12/99 - All trades =================
 Test #      1 of    1                       Space bar to toggle display

 Total net profit        $14,607.75
 Gross profit            $20,747.00  Gross loss              $-6,139.25

 Total # of trades              27  Percent profitable            77%
 Number winning trades          21  Number losing trades            6

 Largest winning trade    $1,107.00  Largest losing trade    $-1,049.25
 Average winning trade      $987.95  Average losing trade    $-1,023.21
 Ratio avg win/avg loss       0.97  Avg trade (win & loss)     $541.03

 Max consecutive winners        9  Max consecutive losers          3
 Avg # bars in winners          3  Avg # bars in losers            1

 Max closed-out drawdown  $-3,090.00  Max intra-day drawdown  $-3,090.00
 Profit factor                3.38  Max # of contracts held         1
 Account size required    $6,090.00  Return on account             239%

== System Writer Plus ======== Omega Research, Inc. ======= Copyright 1989 ==
```

Reprinted with permission of Omega Research, Inc.

S&P 500 PATTERNS
LONG S&P 500

Pattern Code: US881011-2
Type   Exact
Position: Long S&P 500
Profit Target: 10 points = $2,500
Protective Stop: 10 points = $2,500
Order Entry: Open of Tomorrow, O
Order delay: 0

Logic: C(0) > C(3) and C(2) > C(1) and C(1) > C(0)

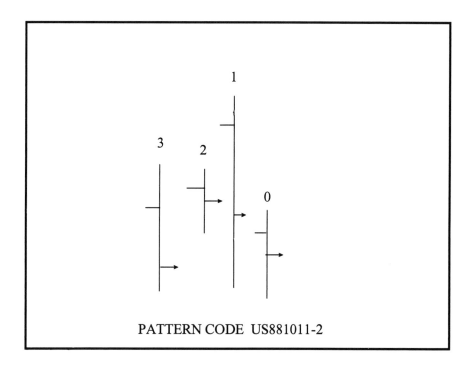

PATTERN CODE US881011-2

S&P 500 PATTERNS
LONG S&P 500

Pattern Code: US881011-2

Historical Performance Results
Period 2/15/83 - 1/7/99

```
HISTORICAL RESULTS : Performance Summary              Model : US TO SP
 Trades   Equity   Chart   Highlights   View-model   Options
Summary, Detailed, Listing

================= SP              12/99 - All trades ================
 Test #     1 of    1                      Space bar to toggle display

 Total net profit        $58,965.00
 Gross profit           $118,229.00  Gross loss              $-59,264.00

 Total # of trades           70      Percent profitable          67%
 Number winning trades       47      Number losing trades         23

 Largest winning trade  $3,957.00    Largest losing trade    $-3,843.00
 Average winning trade  $2,515.51    Average losing trade    $-2,576.70
 Ratio avg win/avg loss      0.98    Avg trade (win & loss)     $842.36

 Max consecutive winners      9      Max consecutive losers        3
 Avg # bars in winners       13      Avg # bars in losers          9

 Max closed-out drawdown $-7,626.00  Max intra-day drawdown  $-7,626.00
 Profit factor               1.99    Max # of contracts held       1
 Account size required  $17,626.00   Return on account           334%

= System Writer Plus ======= Omega Research, Inc. ======= Copyright 1989 =
```

Reprinted with permission of Omega Research, Inc.

203

SWISS FRANC PATTERNS
SHORT SILVER

Pattern Code: SF850419-2
Type   Exact
Position: Short COMEX Silver
Profit Target: 20 points = $1,000
Protective Stop: 20 points = $1,000
Order Entry: Open of Tomorrow, O
Order delay: 0

Logic: L(1) > L(2) and H(1) > H(0) and H(2) > L(1) and
       H(0) > L(0) and L(0) > H(2)

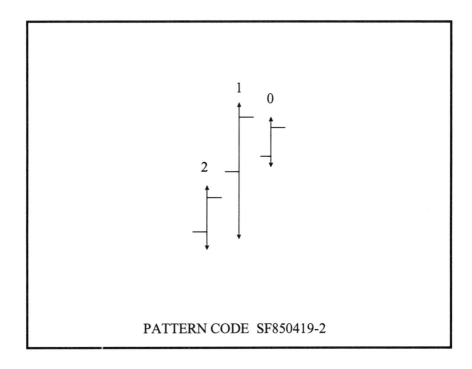

PATTERN CODE SF850419-2

SWISS FRANC PATTERNS
SHORT SILVER

Pattern Code: SF850419-2

Historical Performance Results
Period 2/15/83 - 1/7/99

```
HISTORICAL RESULTS : Performance Summary                    Model : SI
Trades   Equity   Chart   Highlights   View-model   Options
Summary, Detailed, Listing

========================= SI           12/99 - All trades =========
  Test #      1 of    1                      Space bar to toggle display

  Total net profit         $13,963.00
  Gross profit             $24,143.00  Gross loss              $-10,180.00

  Total # of trades               34  Percent profitable              70%
  Number winning trades           24  Number losing trades            10

  Largest winning trade     $1,257.00  Largest losing trade     $-1,018.00
  Average winning trade     $1,005.96  Average losing trade     $-1,018.00
  Ratio avg win/avg loss         0.99  Avg trade (win & loss)      $410.68

  Max consecutive winners          9  Max consecutive losers           2
  Avg # bars in winners           10  Avg # bars in losers             6

  Max closed-out drawdown  $-2,119.00  Max intra-day drawdown   $-2,611.00
  Profit factor                  2.37  Max # of contracts held          1
  Account size required     $5,611.00  Return on account              248%

== System Writer Plus ======== Omega Research, Inc. ======== Copyright 1989 ==
```

Reprinted with permission of Omega Research, Inc.

INDEX

207

identification algorithm, 86
inter-market, 79
matched, 75
proportional, 75
search, 83
split, 77
split-matched, 79
p-Indicator, 54; 120; 124; calculation, 123
    characteristics, 123
    construction, 121
    definition, 120

Q

quarterly returns, 43

R

risk, 101
    constant, 102
    full, 117
    reduced, 117
    variable, 102
Robbins Trading Company, 54

S

short term trading, 8
simulation, 28
Slippage, 6
statistics, 29
stochastic process, 25
symbolic mathematics manipulation,
    99

T

T-Bond Futures, 39
technical trading methods, 14
temporal aggregation, 35

trading signals
    clustered, 112

coincident, 110
successive, 109
Trading Time Frame, 5
trend following, 113

V

visual search, 56

W

World Cup Championship of Futures
    Trading, 54

Reader Service Information

More information can be obtained as follows:

Web Site: www.tradingpatterns.com

By Fax: (212) 898-9076

By e-mail: mharris@tradingpatterns.com

By mail: Address letters to:
                          Mike Harris
                          1204 Third Avenue
                          Suite 251
                          New York, NY 10021

Please include your name and telephone or fax number.

WWW.TRADINGPATTERNS.COM

TRADING PATTERNS

| Home | About Us | Overview | Products | Publications | Contact |

A UNIQUE SERVICE FOR STOCK AND FUTURES TRADERS

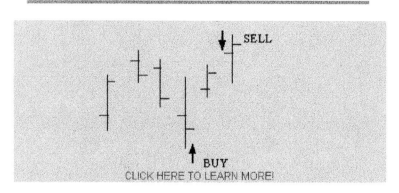

CLICK HERE TO LEARN MORE!

**IF YOU ARE A DAY TRADER OR A SHORT TERM
TRADER, FIND OUT HOW YOU CAN USE PRICE
PATTERNS TO PROFIT FROM THE STOCK AND
FUTURES MARKETS!**

Please contact our webmaster with questions or comments.